UNSTOPPABLE US

VOL. 1 HOW HUMANS TOOK OVER THE WORLD

Yuval Noah Harari

UNSTOPPABLE US

VOL. 1 HOW HUMANS TOOK OVER THE WORLD

Illustrated by Ricard Zaplana Ruiz

BRIGHT MATTER BOOKS

NEW YORK

All rights reserved. Published in the United States by Bright Matter Books,
an imprint of Random House Children's Books, a division of
Penguin Random House LLC, New York.

Bright Matter Books and the colophon are trademarks of
Penguin Random House LLC.

Visit us on the Web! rhcbooks.com

Educators and librarians, for a variety of teaching tools,
visit us at RHTeachersLibrarians.com

Library of Congress Cataloging-in-Publication Data is available upon request.
ISBN 978-0-593-64346-4 (trade)
ISBN 978-0-593-64352-5 (lib. bdg.)
ISBN 978-0-593-64347-1 (ebook)

The text of this book is set in 12-point Neutraface.
Interior design by April Ward
Cover art and interior illustrations by Ricard Zaplana Ruiz

Printed in the United States of America
October 2022
10 9 8 7 6 5 4 3 2 1
First Edition

C.H. Beck & dtv:
Editors: Susanne Stark, Sebastian Ullrich

Sapienship Storytelling:
Production and management: Itzik Yahav
Management and editing: Naama Avital
Marketing and PR: Naama Wartenburg
Editing and project management: Nina Zivy
Research assistant: Jason Parry
Copy editing: Adriana Hunter
Diversity consulting: Slava Greenberg
Design: Hanna Shapiro
sapienship.co

To all beings—those gone, those living,
and those still to come. Our ancestors made
the world what it is. We can decide
what the world will become.

CONTENTS

TIMELINE OF
HISTORY

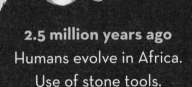

2.5 million years ago
Humans evolve in Africa.
Use of stone tools.

2 million years ago
Evolution of different
kinds of humans

6 million years ago
Last common
ancestor of humans
and chimpanzees

1.5 million years ago
Earliest use of fire

50,000 years ago
Sapiens spread across Australia. Extinction of big Australian animals.

40,000 years ago
Development of art

70,000 years ago
Emergence of storytelling. Sapiens leave Africa in large numbers.

35,000 years ago
Extinction of Neanderthals. Sapiens are the last surviving kind of human.

300,000 years ago
Sapiens evolve in Africa.

400,000 years ago
Neanderthals evolve in Europe and the Middle East.

15,000 years ago
Sapiens spread across the Americas. Extinction of the big American animals.

WHAT ARE HUMANS
ALL ABOUT?

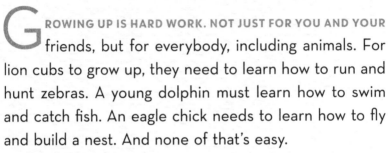

GROWING UP IS HARD WORK. NOT JUST FOR YOU AND YOUR friends, but for everybody, including animals. For lion cubs to grow up, they need to learn how to run and hunt zebras. A young dolphin must learn how to swim and catch fish. An eagle chick needs to learn how to fly and build a nest. And none of that's easy.

But growing up is even harder for humans because we're not sure what we need to learn. Lions run and hunt zebras, dolphins swim and catch fish, eagles fly and build nests—what do humans do?

When you grow up, you might drive a race car faster than any lion can run. You might sail a ship farther than any dolphin can swim. You might pilot an airplane higher than any eagle can fly. You might do a million other things that animals can hardly even imagine. Like invent a computer game, discover a new kind of medicine, lead an expedition to Mars, or sit at home all day and watch TV. Humans have so many options! That's why being a human is really confusing.

But no matter what you end up doing, it's good to know why humans have so many options in the first place. It's because we rule planet Earth.

Planet Earth was once ruled by many different animals. Lions, bears, and elephants ruled the land. Dolphins, whales, and sharks ruled the sea. Eagles, owls, and vultures ruled the sky. But now we humans rule everything: the land, the sea, and the sky. Wherever we go in our cars, ships, and airplanes, the lions, dolphins, and eagles need to move aside—and fast! Animals can't stop us from building highways through their forests. They can't stop us from building dams across their rivers. And they can't stop us from polluting the oceans and skies.

In fact, we humans are now so powerful that the fate of all other animals depends on us. The only reason lions, dolphins, and eagles still exist is because we allow them to. If humans wanted to get rid of all the lions, dolphins, and eagles in the world, we could make it happen by next year.

That's a lot of power, and it can be used in good ways or bad ways. To be a good human being, you need to understand the power you have and what to do with it.

And for that, you need to know how we got our power in the first place.

We humans aren't strong like lions, we don't swim as well as dolphins, and we definitely don't have wings! So how did we end up ruling the planet? The answer to that is one of the strangest tales you'll ever hear.

AND it's a true story.

1

HUMANS ARE
ANIMALS

WE USED TO
BE WILD

OUR STORY STARTS MILLIONS OF YEARS AGO. BACK THEN, humans were just ordinary animals. People didn't live in houses, didn't go to work or to school, and didn't have cars, computers, or supermarkets. They lived in the wild, they climbed trees to pick fruit, they sniffed around looking for mushrooms, and they ate worms, snails, and frogs.

The other animals—giraffes, zebras, and baboons, for instance—weren't afraid of humans and didn't pay them much attention. Nobody imagined that one day humans would fly to the moon, make atom bombs, and write books, like the one you're reading now.

At first, humans didn't even know how to make tools. Sometimes they used stones to crack nuts. But they didn't have bows and arrows, spears, or knives. Humans were relatively weak animals, and whenever a lion or a bear appeared, humans had to run away—and fast!

Nowadays, a lot of kids still wake up in the middle

3

of the night, frightened that there's a monster under the bed. This is a memory from millions of years ago. In the past, there really were monsters that sneaked up on children in the night. If you heard a noise in the dark, it could have been a lion coming to eat you. If you quickly climbed to the top of a tree, you survived. But if you went back to sleep, the lion ate you.

Sometimes, when lions killed a giraffe and ate it, people would watch from a safe distance. They wanted some meat for themselves, but they were too afraid to come close. Even after the lions left, the humans still didn't dare approach. Because the hyenas had moved in to eat the leftovers—and humans were afraid to pick a fight with that quarrelsome bunch. Finally, when all the other animals had gone, the humans tiptoed carefully to the carcass to look for scraps . . . but the only thing left was bare bones. So they shrugged and went off in search of figs.

Then one human had a great idea. She took a stone and used it to crack open a bone. Inside, she found the marrow—that's the juicy stuff in the middle of bones. She ate the marrow and thought it was delicious. Other people saw what she had done and copied her. Soon everyone was using stones to crack bones and eat marrow. Humans finally had something that only they knew how to do!

Each animal has its own special talents: spiders weave webs and catch flies, bees build hives and produce honey, and woodpeckers extract grubs from tree trunks. Some animals have very weird talents. Take cleaner

4

fish, for example. These small fish follow sharks around, waiting for the sharks to eat. Once a shark has had a little tuna snack, he opens his mouth wide, and all the cleaner fish swim inside to clean up bits of tuna stuck between the shark's teeth. The shark gets free dental care, and the cleaner fish get a good meal. Somehow, sharks recognize the cleaner fish and never eat them by mistake.

Now ancient humans also had their special thing: they knew how to use stones to crack open bones so they could eat the marrow inside. Even more important, **humans learned that making tools is a good idea.**

They started using sticks and stones to make all kinds of other tools. Not just for cracking open bones, but for prizing oysters off rocks, for digging up wild onions and carrots, and for hunting small animals like lizards and birds.

Eventually, humans discovered a tool far more amazing than sticks and stones: they discovered how to use fire! Fire is ferocious and terrifying. When a lion eats a zebra, he's no longer hungry, so he lies down and sleeps. But when a fire eats one tree, it only gets hungrier, and leaps wildly from tree to tree. It can eat an entire forest in a day—leaving nothing but ash. If you try to touch or hold fire to stop it from spreading, it will burn you too. So all animals are afraid of fire. They're even more afraid of fire than they are of lions. In fact, even lions are afraid of fire.

But some ancient humans started taking an interest in fire. If only they could use it the same way they used sticks and stones . . .

Do you sometimes like to just sit and stare into a fire, watching the flames dance? That's another memory from ancient humans. At first, humans approached fire very cautiously, observing it from a distance. Perhaps they discovered that if lightning set fire to a tree, they could sit around it and enjoy light and warmth. Better still, as long as the tree burned, no dangerous animal dared approach them.

COOKS HAVE
BIG BRAINS

Humans watched fire again and again and came to understand it better. They realized that even though it was wild and ferocious, it did obey some rules. They could

befriend it. They pushed a long stick toward a burning tree, and when the tip of the stick caught fire, they pulled it back again. They now had fire on a stick. The fire didn't burn them, but they could burn anything they touched with their stick. This was so useful! They could take fire with them from place to place to stay warm and scare lions.

But there was still one big problem: people didn't know how to start a fire. Waiting for lightning to strike could be very frustrating. You could sit near a tree for a whole year—and still no lightning would strike that tree. And if a lion was chasing you, you couldn't even wait two seconds.

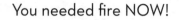

You needed fire NOW!

Eventually, humans figured out how to solve this problem. One way to create fire was to knock a flint stone against another kind of stone called pyrite. If you struck the pyrite very hard, it produced a spark, and if you directed the spark toward dry leaves, they sometimes caught fire and started to burn.

Another way was to find a large piece of dry wood, carve a hole in it, and put dry leaves inside the hole. Then you sharpened one end of a twig, put the sharp end into the hole, and twisted the twig between your hands very quickly for a couple of minutes.

Friction caused the end of the twig to get hotter and hotter, until it eventually set light to the dry leaves. Smoke started to drift out of the hole, then a flame leapt up. Fire! Now, if a lion showed up, you just needed to wave your fire stick, and the lion would run away.

The way humans used fire made them unique. Almost all animals depend on their own bodies for power: the strength of their muscles, the size of their teeth, or the sharpness of their claws. But thanks to fire, humans

8

gained control of a limitless source of power that had nothing to do with their bodies. A single weak human with a fire stick could burn down an entire forest in a matter of hours, destroying thousands of trees and killing thousands of animals.

But the greatest thing about fire wasn't that it drove away lions or gave people warmth and light. No, the greatest thing about fire was that **it meant ancient humans could start cooking.**

Before humans had fire, it took a long time and a lot of effort to eat raw food. You had to break it into little pieces and chew it for a while, and even then, your stomach had to work very hard to digest it. So humans needed big teeth, a big stomach, and a lot of patience. **Once humans had fire, eating became much easier.** Cooking made the food soft, so it required far less time and effort to eat and digest. As a result, humans started to change: they had smaller teeth, smaller stomachs . . . and much more free time!

You can test this for yourself. Next time someone is cooking potatoes, ask to taste a raw one. Wait, don't eat it! Just lick a tiny piece. You'll probably spit it out and want to rinse your mouth. It's hard and yucky! But cooked potatoes are delicious. In your kitchen you most likely cook potatoes on a stove, in an oven, or in a microwave, without actually making a fire. But all cooking started with an open fire. So if you enjoy baked potatoes or fries, you've got your friend fire to thank for them.

Some scientists even suggest it was cooking that made it possible for the human brain to start growing. What's the connection between cooking and brains?

Well, when humans spent a lot of time and energy chewing food with their big teeth and digesting it with their big stomachs, there wasn't much energy left for the brain. So the first humans, the ones with the big stomachs, had small brains. Once they started cooking, that all changed: humans could spend far less energy chewing and digesting and had more energy to feed big brains. Their stomachs shrank, their brains grew, and people got smarter.

But we shouldn't exaggerate the difference that this made. Yes, ancient humans were now smarter. They could make tools, start fires, even sometimes hunt a zebra or a giraffe. And they could protect themselves better from lions and bears. But that was all. Humans were still just another animal. They definitely didn't rule the world.

DIFFERENT KINDS OF
HUMAN

Today, people around the world may look different and speak different languages, but we're actually all the same. Whether you go to China or Italy, to Greenland or South Africa, you find the same kinds of humans everywhere.

Of course, there are differences in things like hair color and skin color between—for example—Chinese, Italians, Greenlanders, and South Africans, but **underneath the skin we all have similar bodies, similar brains, and similar abilities.** Chinese people can learn Italian, Greenlanders can play football with South Africans, and everybody can build a spaceship together.

It's quite strange that there's just one kind of human all over the world. After all, in every country there are different kinds of ants, snakes, or bears. In icy Greenland, there are polar bears; in the Canadian mountains, grizzly bears; in the woodlands of Romania, brown bears; and in the bamboo forests of China, panda bears. **So why is there just one type of human in all these places?**

Well, for a very long time, our planet was actually home to many different kinds of humans. In various parts of the world, humans had to deal with different animals, plants, and climates. Some humans lived in high mountains with lots of snow, and some lived on tropical seashores with lots of sun. Some humans flourished in the desert, some in swamps. For more than a million years, as humans adapted to the unique conditions of each area, they gradually became more and more different—just like the bears.

So why is it that today all humans are the same kind? What happened to the other kinds? A terrible catastrophe killed them, and only our kind of humans remained. What was this catastrophe? **That's a big secret that people don't like to talk about.** We'll discuss it in a moment, but first let's get to know some of the other kinds of humans that once lived in different parts of the world.

AN ISLAND OF
SMALL HUMANS

Let's begin our family tour on the small island of Flores, in what is today Indonesia. About a million years ago, the sea level around Flores Island was lower. Many places that are now covered by water were dry land back then, so Flores was much closer to the mainland. Some curious humans and other animals, like elephants, found it easy to cross over to the island. But when the sea rose, they couldn't get back to the mainland and were stuck on the island.

Flores is a small island, and there wasn't much to eat there. The biggest people and the biggest elephants, who needed a lot of food, died first. **The smaller ones, who needed less food, survived.** When a small man and a small woman had babies together, they had even smaller babies. Of course, not all the babies were exactly the same size—some were small, some even smaller. Because

14

there still wasn't much food, it was again the smaller ones who survived. And that's how, from generation to generation, both the people and the elephants of Flores Island became smaller and smaller. Adult Floresians were no more than three feet tall and weighed about fifty-five pounds. But they knew how to use tools and even hunt the small elephants.

The way these humans and elephants gradually became smaller is an example of evolution. Evolution explains not only where the small people and elephants of Flores Island came from but where all animals and plants came from. It explains why giraffes have such long necks, why foxes are so smart, and why skunks smell so terrible.

When giraffes compete to eat the leaves on trees, the giraffe with the longest neck can reach the highest leaves.

She gets more food, so she has more babies—and her babies will also have long necks. When foxes compete to hunt prey, the smartest foxes are the most successful, so they have more cubs, and their cubs are smart too. And when a fox tries to hunt skunks, the fox will probably be disgusted by the smelliest skunk and leave him alone—so the smelliest skunk will survive and make super-stinky baby skunks!

It's important to remember that evolution takes many generations. It took a long time for skunks to become really smelly, and it also took thousands of years for the humans and elephants on Flores Island to become small. It didn't happen overnight like in a fairy tale, when someone drinks a magic potion and immediately becomes tiny, or when a wizard casts a spell and—shazam!—a prince turns into a frog. In fact, it took so much time that nobody noticed the changes. With every generation, the humans and elephants became a little smaller—and since nobody lived for a thousand years, nobody realized what was happening.

This is one of the big laws of life: small changes that nobody notices accumulate over time and become big changes. It happens not only with evolution but with many other things in nature. If you watch water drip onto a solid rock, you might think that the rock is much stronger than the water. The water just flows off the rock without making any difference. But if you could come back thousands of years later, you would see that the water has made a deep hole in the rock. Each single drop makes only a tiny difference, but after millions of drops, it turns out that persistent water is stronger than solid rock.

Or think about growing up. You never see yourself growing when you look in the mirror. You could stand there for an hour, looking very carefully, but you still wouldn't see yourself get taller or your hair get longer. If you look in the mirror every morning, you probably look exactly like yesterday. But in twenty years, you'll look completely different. How does that work? Is there a special day when you take a magic pill, go to sleep, and wake up as an adult? No, you change a little every day, and over the years these tiny changes add up to the grown-up you.

This is how we grow up. This is how water can make a hole in a rock. And this is how the humans on Flores Island became small. Slowly, slowly, step by step.

The small humans lived on Flores for many years, but the catastrophe that killed all the other kinds of humans didn't spare them. So, until recently, nobody knew that they ever existed. Well, almost nobody. Some people on Flores told stories about bands of small humans who once lived deep in the jungle. The locals called them the Ebu Gogo, which means Grandma Eats All, because the little humans in these stories would eat absolutely anything! But most people just dismissed the stories as fairy tales.

And then a few years ago, archaeologists started digging inside a cave on Flores Island. Archaeologists are scientists who dig in all kinds of places, hoping to find clues about the distant past. What they found in that cave on Flores Island was fascinating: very old stone tools, the remains of a campfire, some elephant bones, and the skeletons of several small humans who lived on the island more than 50,000 years ago.

At first the archaeologists thought these were the skeletons of children, but it turned out they were those of adults. So the Ebu Gogo perhaps weren't a fairy tale!

THE HUMAN
FAMILY

While the humans who settled Flores Island became very small, another kind of human was evolving in Europe and many parts of Asia. It was quite cold in those parts, so these humans adapted to a cold climate. Scientists call them the humans from the Neander Valley, or Neanderthals,

Floresian

Neanderthal

Sapiens

because the first evidence of their existence was found in a cave in the Neander Valley in Germany. The Neanderthals were about the same height as we are, but they were heavier and much stronger. They also had bigger brains than we do.

What did Neanderthals do with their big brains? They didn't build cars or airplanes, and they didn't write books. But they did make tools and jewelry and probably lots of other things, too. Maybe they were even better than us at recognizing bird songs or tracking animals—or dancing and dreaming. Maybe . . . and maybe not. We just don't know.

There are many things we don't know about the past, and if we don't know something, it's always best to say: "I don't know." In science, saying "I don't know" is especially

important. It's the first step, because only after you admit that you don't know something can you start searching for the answer. If you claim to already know everything, why bother?

In 2008, archaeologists made another surprising discovery. While exploring the Denisova Cave in Siberia, they found a piece of bone from an ancient human finger. It was from the pinkie of a young girl who lived about 50,000 years ago.

When the archaeologists examined the bone closely, they discovered that **this girl was a previously unknown kind of human.** She wasn't a Neanderthal or a small Floresian, and she was also quite different from us. The archaeologists named the girl and her relatives the Denisovans after the cave where the finger bone was found.

You might wonder how we can know for sure that this finger belonged to an unknown kind of human and not, say, a Neanderthal. Well, each part of our bodies is made of many small cells, which join together to form a nose, a heart, or a finger. Each of these cells contains a copy of a tiny "instruction book" that tells the cell what to do. This instruction book tells some cells to form a nose and others to form a finger. Even your spit, your bones, and the roots of your hairs contain copies of this instruction book—otherwise, your body wouldn't know how to make more spit, more bone, and more hair. **This instruction book is called DNA.**

5'5"

3'6"

You can't see it with the naked eye, but if you take a drop of spit, a piece of bone, or a strand of hair and put it under a very powerful microscope, you can see the DNA curled up inside a cell. And if you use all kinds of special instruments, you can even read the instructions coded in the DNA. If you read the DNA of people with dark skin, you find instructions for making dark skin. The DNA of people with light skin contains instructions for making light skin.

So if you manage to get even a single piece of DNA from someone, you'll know a lot about them, even if

the person lived a long time ago! **DNA can survive for thousands of years** after someone dies, especially in cold, dry places.

The Denisova Cave in Siberia is very cold and very dry. When the archaeologists examined the finger bone that they found there, they managed to extract some DNA from it and read its code. It wasn't like the DNA of any known type of human. And that's how the scientists knew that the people who lived in the Denisova Cave 50,000 years ago belonged to a previously unknown kind of human, different from us, from the Neanderthals, and from the small humans of Flores Island.

Just imagine that sometime in the distant future,

all humans on earth have disappeared, and the world is ruled by super-smart rats. One day, a rat archaeologist might dig in a cave and find your finger! And thanks to your finger alone, the rats would know that humans once lived on earth. So take good care of your fingers.

Many other kinds of humans once lived on earth besides the small Floresians, the Neanderthals, and the Denisovans. We know very little about them because they didn't leave many bones or tools and we can't read their DNA.

WHICH KIND OF
HUMAN ARE YOU?

But there was one kind of ancient human we know a lot about. They were our ancestors from many thousands of years ago. At the time when the small humans lived on Flores Island, the Neanderthals lived in Europe, and the Denisovans were hanging around caves in Siberia, our ancestors lived mostly in Africa.

Scientists call our ancestors *Homo sapiens,* or Sapiens for short. Is it because they lived on Sapiens Island, in Sapiens Valley, or in Sapiens Cave? Not at all. The words *homo* and *sapiens* are Latin. Latin is an old language that few people speak today. Because it's old and complicated, Latin sounds almost like magic, so when scientists want to make something sound very

important, they give it a name in Latin. They do it with diseases, medicines, plants, and animals.

Say a scientist is talking about cats and wants to sound very serious. She wouldn't say *cat*; she would say *Felis catus*, which means "cunning cat" in Latin. And she would call mice *Mus musculus*, which means "mousy mouse" in Latin. If you read "cunning cat hunts mousy mouse" in a book, you might think it was a story for babies. But if you read "*Felis catus* hunts *Mus musculus*" in a book, you'd most likely think it was an important science book.

All the different kinds of human were also given their own fancy Latin names. When scientists talk about Neanderthals and want to sound serious and important, they don't call them Neanderthals but *Homo neanderthalensis*. In Latin, *Homo* means "human" and *neanderthalensis* means "from Neander Valley," so together it means "humans from Neander Valley." And when scientists talk about the small humans from Flores, they certainly don't call them small humans. That would be way too simple! Instead, they call them *Homo floresiensis*, which means "humans from Flores Island."

When scientists were choosing a name for our kind of human, of course they gave us a very respectable Latin name—*Homo sapiens*. But what does it mean? Well, in Latin, the word *sapiens* means "wise." So *Homo sapiens* means "wise humans."

We decided to call ourselves "wise humans," which wasn't very modest of us. Especially as it's not at all clear

that we Sapiens are really any wiser than the other humans were. **But there it is, that's our name—Sapiens.** You are Sapiens, and all your friends and relatives are also Sapiens. All the people in the world today are Sapiens— Germans are Sapiens, Nigerians are Sapiens, Koreans are Sapiens, and Brazilians are Sapiens.

NEXT STOP:
SUPER-SAPIENS

About 100,000 years ago, our Sapiens ancestors lived mainly in Africa. They already looked just like people today—that is, if you gave them a nice haircut and dressed them in jeans and T-shirts instead of animal skins. **But these ancient Sapiens were quite different from us.**

Like all the other humans, Sapiens already had fire and stone tools, so they could frighten away lions and even hunt some big animals. But they didn't know how to sow wheat or ride horses, they didn't know how to build wagons or ships, and they didn't have any villages, let alone big cities. There were also very few of them. In all of Africa, there were probably fewer than 100,000 Sapiens. You could cram all of them into one huge football stadium. **Back then, the most important animal on the planet wasn't Sapiens—not yet.** Maybe it was whales . . . or ants.

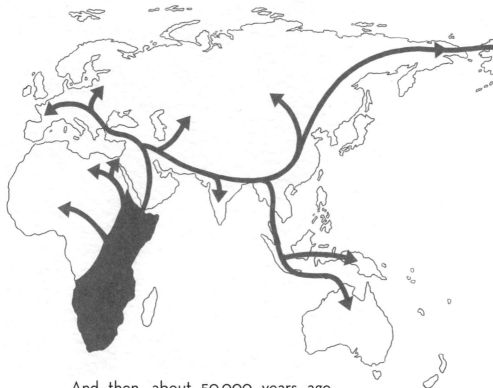

And then, about 50,000 years ago, everything changed. A huge catastrophe hit planet Earth and killed the small Floresians, the Neanderthals, the Denisovans, and all the other kinds of humans—except for the Sapiens. What was this catastrophe? It wasn't an asteroid from outer space. It wasn't a massive volcanic eruption. It wasn't an earthquake. No . . . it was our ancestors themselves.

Around that time, something very strange happened to our ancestors, making them super powerful. Are you wondering what that was? It's actually quite intriguing. But we'll explain it later—like in a good

detective story, you have to read on to get to the bottom of the mystery! For now we'll say only that it had an incredible effect: **Sapiens began spreading all over the world,** and whenever they reached a new valley or island, all the other kinds of humans that lived there quickly disappeared.

For example, when the new super-Sapiens reached Europe, they picked all the pears, ate all the berries, and hunted all the deer. This meant that the local Neanderthals had nothing left to eat, so they died of hunger. And if any Neanderthals tried to stop the Sapiens from taking all the food, the Sapiens probably killed them.

Then our ancestors went to Siberia and took all the food from the Denisovans. And then they went to Flores, and . . . what do you know, soon there wasn't a single small human or small elephant to be found. **And when all the other humans were gone, our ancestors still weren't satisfied.** Although they were now incredibly powerful, they wanted *even more* power and more food, so they sometimes fought one another.

A NEANDERTHAL
IN THE FAMILY

You see, we Sapiens are not very nice animals. We can be cruel to other Sapiens simply because they have a different skin color or speak a different language or practice a different religion. So it's hardly surprising that when our Sapiens ancestors met humans of a completely different kind, like the Neanderthals, they probably didn't treat them well.

But a few years ago, scientists discovered that **at least some of our Sapiens ancestors didn't kill or starve all the other humans they met.** Do you remember DNA— our body's instruction book? Not only can DNA reveal the color of your hair or the shape of your fingers, it can also reveal who your parents are, and who their parents are, and their parents, all the way back for thousands of years. This is because you got your DNA from your parents, who got it from their parents, who got it from theirs.

When scientists began reading the DNA of Neanderthals, they learned something amazing: some people living today got a few of the instructions in their DNA from Neanderthals! That means that even though all people alive today are Sapiens, at least some of us also have a Neanderthal ancestor.

It's quite easy to check whether you have a Neanderthal ancestor. You just need to spit into a test tube and send it to a laboratory. Even a single drop of your spit contains millions of copies of your DNA. The lab can extract your DNA from your spit, and tell you whether parts of it came from a Neanderthal who had children with one of your ancestors 50,000 years ago.

But why would your ancestor want to have children with a Neanderthal? We don't know for sure,

but **maybe they fell in love,** and even if all his friends laughed at him and all her friends warned her not to date a Neanderthal, love overcame these obstacles.

Or perhaps a band of Sapiens adopted a baby Neanderthal orphan after all her relatives died. Maybe on another occasion some Sapiens captured a Neanderthal girl, and even though she wanted to go back to her people, they forced her to go with them. If young Neanderthals grew up among Sapiens, they might have gone on to have children with a Sapiens partner. But these seem to have been rare events. **In most cases, our ancestors drove away all the Neanderthals they met.**

WHAT
IF . . . ?

It's fascinating to imagine how the world would look if our ancestors had been nicer and had allowed the Neanderthals and the Floresians to go on living and developing. **What would it be like if these other humans were still among us today?**

Maybe there would be some tough Neanderthal kids on your school track team. Maybe your next-door neighbors would be small immigrants from Flores. And what about politics and religion? Would Denisovans be allowed to vote in elections? Would priests agree to bless the marriage of a Neanderthal and a Sapiens? Could a Neanderthal be a priest, a rabbi, or an imam?

Would you like to have a Neanderthal friend?

If the other humans had survived alongside us, maybe it would even have changed the way we see ourselves. **Today, most humans think we're very special creatures.** If you try to tell them that humans are animals, they often get seriously upset because they think we're completely different from animals.

People might think this because once all the other kinds of humans disappeared, there was nothing like us anywhere on Earth. It was easy to imagine that we Sapiens weren't like other animals. But if the Neanderthals or the Floresians had survived, it would have been much harder for us to think of ourselves as unique.

32

Maybe that's why our ancestors got rid of all the other humans.

But how did our ancestors manage to overcome the other humans? The Neanderthals were stronger than them, the Denisovans were better adapted to cold places than they were, and the small humans of Flores needed less food than they did . . . and yet our ancestors ended up conquering the whole of planet Earth. What was their superpower?

2

THE SAPIENS' SUPERPOWER

BANANA
ADVENTURES

So, WHAT DO YOU THINK? WHAT HAPPENED 50,000 YEARS ago? What superpower did Sapiens get that allows us to rule the planet today? The answer isn't obvious. Superman, Spider-Man, Wonder Woman, and all the other comic superheroes are powerful because they're strong, fast, and brave. But Sapiens weren't stronger, faster, or braver than Neanderthals—or plenty of other animals, for that matter. In a fight with a wolf, a crocodile, or a chimpanzee, a Sapiens would have very little chance of winning. Even an old grandma chimpanzee could beat the world boxing champion.

The only reason we can scare away wolves and lock chimpanzees in zoos is that we cooperate in very large numbers. One human can't defeat one chimpanzee, but a thousand humans can achieve incredible things that chimpanzees can't even dream of. And it's thanks to our secret superpower that we can cooperate better than any other animal. We can even cooperate with complete strangers.

Take, for example, the last piece of fruit you ate. Maybe it was a banana. Where did that banana come from? If you were a chimp, you'd have to go to the forest and pick a banana yourself. But because you're a human, you usually rely on help from strangers. Very few people pick their own bananas. In most cases, someone you've never met and never will meet grew this banana thousands of miles from you. Then other strangers put it on a truck, a train, or perhaps a ship and transported it to your local store. Then you went to the store, chose your banana, took it to the cashier, and gave the cashier some money. And that's how you got your banana.

How many people touched that banana before you bought it? How many of these people do you know personally? Maybe you don't know any of them . . . but they helped you get your banana.

Or think about your school. How many people make up a school? First of all, you need lots of students.

Without them, the school would be pointless! How many kids are there at your school? Then you need teachers. Try to count how many teachers your school has. And there are the people who built the school, the people who clean it, the people who serve food in its cafeteria, the people who generate electricity so you have light in the classroom, the people who wrote and printed all the textbooks, and many, many others. So, all in all, how many people does it take to make a school? And how many of them do you know personally?

All the big achievements of humankind, such as flying to the moon, were the result of cooperation between hundreds of thousands of people. In 1969, Neil Armstrong was the first man to set foot on the moon. He got there by flying in a spaceship, but he didn't build the spaceship himself.

Countless people cooperated to build the spaceship: miners extracted iron from the earth to build it, engineers designed it, mathematicians calculated the best course to the moon, technicians made special boots so that Armstrong could walk on the moon, and farmers grew bananas so that the astronauts would have something to eat in space.

Eagles fly because they have wings. Humans fly because they know how to cooperate in large numbers. This is what makes us so powerful. We can cooperate with thousands of strangers to get bananas or build a school or fly to the moon. Chimpanzees can't do that. They don't have stores where they can buy bananas that grew on the other side of the world. They don't have

schools where hundreds of young chimps study together. They don't fly anywhere, certainly not to the moon.

Chimpanzees can't do all these things because they cooperate only in small numbers, and they rarely cooperate with strangers. Say you were a chimp and wanted to cooperate with another chimp. You would have to know that chimp personally: What kind of chimp is he? Is he friendly or nasty? Is he reliable? How could you cooperate with the chimp if you didn't know him?

If you made a list of everyone you know really well, how many people would be on it? Not people you see on television, but people you actually meet. People who know your secrets—and you know theirs. If a bear chased you up a tree, who would come help you?

If you're like most people, **your list will have fewer than 150 names.** Scientists have asked a lot of people to make lists like this, and they've found that it's basically impossible for humans to form strong personal connections with more than about 150 individuals.

Now try to count all the people you come across in one day. All the people who pass you on the street. All the people who travel on the bus with you. All the people who go to school with you. All the people who shop in the same store. All the people who attend a soccer game with you. **How many do you think there will be?**

If you live in a big city like New York or Tokyo, you'll probably count thousands of people. Isn't that amazing? Even though you really know just 150 people, you get to see thousands of strangers every time you go to a big shopping mall, a sports stadium, or a train station. If you tried to cram thousands of chimpanzees into these places, the result would be total chaos. But thousands of humans squeeze into them every day, and most of the time they all behave in a perfectly orderly way.

And that's how our Sapiens ancestors overcame the Neanderthals and all the other kinds of humans thousands of years ago. Our ancestors were the only ones who knew how to cooperate in large numbers, even with strangers. More people cooperating meant more ideas about how to make tools, find food, and heal wounds.

Neanderthals learned stuff and got help only from a

few close friends and relatives, but **Sapiens could rely on lots of people they didn't know well.** So even though a single Sapiens wasn't smarter than a single Neanderthal, Sapiens became much better at inventing tools and hunting animals. And if things ever came to a fight, 500 Sapiens could easily defeat 50 Neanderthals.

WHY ANTS HAVE QUEENS
BUT NO LAWYERS

There's only one other type of animal that can cooperate in very large numbers: social insects, such as ants, bees, and termites. **Just as we live in villages and cities, so ants and bees live in colonies and hives** that sometimes contain many thousands of individuals. Thousands of ants cooperate to get food, take care of their young, build bridges, and even fight wars.

Yet there is one big difference between humans and ants: **ants know how to organize themselves in only one way.** For example, there's a type of ant called the harvester ant. If you watch a colony of harvester ants anywhere in the world, you'll find that all the colonies are organized in exactly the same way. In every colony, the ants divide themselves into five groups: foragers, build-ers, warriors, nurses, and queens.

The foragers go out to harvest grain and hunt small insects, which they carry back to the colony for food. The builders dig tunnels and build the colony. The warriors protect the colony and fight against other ant armies. The nurses take care of the baby ants. And the queen rules the colony and lays eggs to make more baby ants.

This is the only way these ants know how to organize themselves. A colony will never rebel against its queen and start having elections to choose an ant president. The builders and foragers never go on strike to demand higher wages. The warriors never decide to sign a peace treaty with neighboring colonies. The nurses never quit their jobs to become lawyers, sculptors, or opera singers. They never invent new foods, new weapons, or new games like tennis. Harvester ants today live exactly as they did thousands of years ago.

In contrast to ants, **we humans constantly change how we cooperate with one another.**

We invent new games, we design new clothes, we create new jobs, and we have political revolutions. Three hundred years ago, people played with bows and arrows to hit a target. Today, we play computer games to reach a top score. Three hundred years ago, most people were farmers. Today, we work as bus drivers, dog groomers, computer programmers, and personal trainers. Three hundred years ago, most countries were ruled by kings and queens. Today, most countries are ruled by parliaments and presidents.

So we Sapiens conquered the world because we can cooperate in very large numbers, like ants, and can constantly change the way we cooperate, which helps us invent new things. Is that our superpower? Not quite. To understand our unique Sapiens superpower, we need to raise one last question: **How did our ancestors learn to cooperate** in large numbers in the first place, and how come we can constantly change our behavior? The answer to that is our real superpower. What do you think it is?

ZOMBIES, VAMPIRES, AND FAIRIES

The truth is, you might find the answer a little disappointing. When you saw the word "superpower," maybe you expected something like reading minds, seeing the future, or becoming invisible. But you know humans can't read minds, see the future, or become invisible. So it can't be any of those. Our superpower must be something we all have, right?

Actually, our superpower is something we use all the time. We just don't think of it as a superpower. Many people even see it as a weakness. It is—drumroll, please!—our ability to dream up stuff that isn't really there and to tell all kinds of imaginary stories. We're the only animals that can invent and believe in legends, fairy tales, and myths.

Of course, other animals can communicate. When a chimpanzee sees a lion approaching, he can shout (in chimp language), "Look out! There's a lion coming!" and

all the chimpanzees run away. And if a chimpanzee sees a banana, he can say, "Look, there's a banana over there! Let's get it!" But chimpanzees can't invent things that they never saw or tasted or touched, like unicorns or zombies.

Just like chimps, we Sapiens can use language to describe what we see and taste and touch, but we can also invent stories about things that don't exist, like fairies and vampires. Chimps can't do that. Even Neanderthals couldn't do it.

How did Sapiens get this strange ability? We're not sure. One explanation is that something in the Sapiens' DNA instruction book changed by mistake. Maybe two parts of the brain that used to be completely separate started connecting. Maybe this mistake made the Sapiens' brains start producing seriously strange stories. Mistakes can sometimes create wonderful new things. And this mistake didn't happen in the Neanderthals' instruction book, so Neanderthals couldn't invent and believe stories.

Maybe . . . and maybe not. We don't really know. Scientists are still investigating this question.

But the really important question isn't how Sapiens got this ability to tell stories, but what telling stories is good for. **And why call this a superpower?** So what if Sapiens could invent fairy tales and Neanderthals couldn't? How do fairy tales help you in a wild forest? If a genie came out of a bottle and offered you a special power, would you choose the power to become invisible or to invent stories about fairies?

In fact, you might think that believing in fairy tales could be a problem. If Sapiens went to the forest looking for imaginary fairies, unicorns, and spirits while Neanderthals went looking for real deer, nuts, and mushrooms, shouldn't the Neanderthals have survived better?

Well, the useful thing about stories is that no matter how ridiculous they are, they help large numbers of people cooperate. **If thousands of people believe in the same story, then they'll all follow the same rules,** which means they can cooperate effectively, even with strangers. Thanks to stories, Sapiens cooperate much better than Neanderthals or chimpanzees or ants.

THE GREAT
LION SPIRIT

Let's say a Sapiens tells everyone this story: "There's a Great Lion Spirit that lives above the clouds. If you obey the Great Lion Spirit, then when you die, you'll go to the land of the spirits, and you'll have all the bananas you can eat. But if you disobey the Great Lion Spirit, a big lion will come and eat you!"

Of course, this story isn't true at all. But if a thousand people believe it, they'll all start doing whatever the story tells them to do. **Then those thousand people can easily cooperate, even if they don't know one another.**

If you say, "The Great Lion Spirit wants everyone to stand on one foot," then a thousand people will stand on one foot!

If you say, "The Great Lion Spirit wants everyone to wear an empty coconut shell

on their head," then a thousand people will wear empty coconut shells on their heads! (Which is very helpful because then it's easy to tell who believes in the Great Lion Spirit and who doesn't.)

If you say that the Great Lion Spirit wants everyone to come together to fight the Neanderthals or build a temple, then a thousand people will cooperate to fight the Neanderthals or build a temple.

If you say, "The Great Lion Spirit wants everyone to give a banana to the priest in the temple, and in return, when they die, they'll receive lots and lots of bananas in the land of the spirits," then a thousand people will bring bananas to the priest. And the priest will have a mountain of bananas!

This is something only we Sapiens can do. You could never persuade a chimpanzee to give you a banana by promising him that when he dies, he'll go to chimpanzee heaven and have all the bananas he can eat. No chimp would ever believe you—only Sapiens believe stories like that. And that's why we rule the world, whereas poor chimps are locked up in zoos.

Does this all sound strange to you? Do you find it hard to believe that stories control the world? Just **look at how all the grown-ups around you behave.** They do some interesting things, don't they?

Some people wear all kinds of hats because they believe that a god likes these hats very much. Other people don't eat certain foods because they believe that a god said not to eat them. Some go fight people on the

other side of the world because they believe that a god told them to. Others give lots of money to construct a big building because they believe that a god wants it.

Their children might ask, "Why do we need this building? Why do we have to wear these hats? Why do we have to fight people on the other side of the world?" And the parents tell them the stories that all the grown-ups believe so that the children start believing them too.

We're not sure exactly when Sapiens first started telling stories. But it was a very long time ago, when the small Floresians and the Neanderthals still lived on Earth alongside our ancestors. We don't know what stories they told back then. Maybe they told stories about the Great

Lion Spirit. Maybe the Great Lion Spirit looked like a human with the head of a lion.

In the Stadel Cave in Germany, archaeologists actually found a statue that had a human body with a lion's head. This statue was carved by Sapiens about 32,000 years ago. No creature like this ever existed. So the lion-man must have been invented by people who lived in Germany 32,000 years ago. We don't know what story they told about the lion-man, but **if thousands of people all believed it, this helped them cooperate.** And their cooperation helped them push aside the Neanderthals who lived in Germany before they arrived.

Eventually, people stopped believing in the lion-man. His story was forgotten, and the statue was thrown away. And even though archaeologists found the statue, nobody today knows the lion-man story. People now believe other stories instead.

STORIES THAT
GROWN-UPS
BELIEVE

Did you ever go to a park and meet some kids you'd never seen before, and within minutes you were all playing soccer together? How did you do that when you didn't know the other kids? After all, soccer's quite a complicated

game with lots of rules.

Each child might insist on different rules. One kid might argue that the aim of soccer is to stand with both feet on the ball without falling. Whoever can stay standing the longest is soccer champion. Another kid might hide the ball and say that the winner is whoever finds the ball first. Two other children might just pick up the ball and start throwing it back and forth, saying that this is how they play soccer and there isn't a winner at all. Why should every game be about winning, anyway?

If everyone followed different rules, how could you ever play soccer together?

Luckily, most of the time you don't have problems like this **because most kids believe the same story** about soccer. Everyone accepts that the aim of soccer is to kick the ball into the goal. Everyone accepts that you can only touch the ball with your feet, never your hands, unless you're the goalkeeper. Everyone accepts that you can never kick another player.

Everyone accepts that the pitch has boundaries, and the moment the ball crosses a boundary, it is out and passes to the other team.

But why do all kids accept these rules? Well, it's because their parents and teachers told them the story of soccer. Perhaps they saw their older brothers and sisters play soccer, and they probably even watched famous people like Lionel Messi and Megan Rapinoe play soccer on television.

In exactly the same way, grown-ups can play very complicated games because they all believe the same stories and follow the same rules. **One of the most interesting games grown-ups play is called "corporation."** It's way more complicated than soccer.

Have you heard of this game? Do you know any famous corporations? You've heard of McDonald's, right? Well, that's a corporation. So are Coca-Cola, and Google, and Facebook, Disney, Toyota, Mercedes-Benz, and Ford. If your family has a car, that car was made by a corporation. If you eat cereal for breakfast or chocolate for dessert, look at the packaging. You'll probably see the name and the logo of the corporation that made what you're eating.

Perhaps someone in your family works for a corporation. Do you know which one?

But what exactly is a corporation? Is it something you can see, hear, touch, or smell? You would think so because we hear about corporations and the things they do all the time. They hire people, they fire people, they pollute the environment, or they invent something that might save the world. They must be real, just as a chimpanzee or a banana is real, right? But let's take a closer look at McDonald's, for example. What exactly is McDonald's?

Well, it isn't the burgers and fries that so many kids love to eat. McDonald's makes burgers, but McDonald's isn't the burgers themselves. If Godzilla showed up and

ate all the burgers, what would happen to the McDonald's Corporation? Not much. It would still be there, and it would just make more burgers.

So maybe McDonald's is the restaurants where you eat the burgers and fries. No, that's not right. McDonald's Corporation has thousands of restaurants, but that doesn't mean it *is* the restaurants. A big earthquake might destroy all the McDonald's restaurants, but that wouldn't destroy the McDonald's Corporation. McDonald's would just build new restaurants and go on making burgers and fries.

So maybe McDonald's is the people who work in the restaurants? The managers, cooks, servers, and cleaners. No, that's not right either. Let's say that all the workers left their jobs and went to work at Burger King instead. McDonald's wouldn't disappear. It would just hire other people to do these jobs. All the workers would be different, but McDonald's would remain the same.

Well then, McDonald's must be the people who hire all the workers, and decide how much money to give them, and where to open new restaurants. These people are the owners of McDonald's. When McDonald's sells lots of burgers and makes lots of money, these owners become rich.

But the owners of McDonald's change all the time. In the beginning, McDonald's was owned by just one family. Can you guess what their name was?

Right, it was the McDonald family. Richard and Maurice McDonald opened the first McDonald's

restaurant in 1940 and
named it after themselves. But Richard
and Maurice McDonald died many years ago, and the
McDonald's Corporation is still here. Did their children
inherit McDonald's? No, because Richard and Maurice
McDonald sold it to other people long before they died.
And these other people sold it to other people. Who sold
it to other people.

Today, thousands of people own the McDonald's
Corporation between them. Each person owns just a small
part of it. **These small parts are called "shares,"** and if
you wanted, you too could buy a share of McDonald's.
One share would cost you about $250 today. Then you'd
be one of the owners of McDonald's.

And if you bought lots and lots of shares, you could

be one of the biggest owners of McDonald's, and then you could decide to open a McDonald's on your street, or make a totally new kind of burger out of celery, or give workers twice as much money every month. But would it mean that you *were* McDonald's? Not at all. People buy and sell shares of McDonald's all the time, the owners change again and again, and yet McDonald's stays the same. The McDonald's Corporation is not the people who own it.

So we still don't know what McDonald's is, do we? Where could you go if you wanted to see, hear, touch, or smell it? The truth is, you just can't. You can look at the restaurants, talk to the cooks, touch the tables, and smell the burgers. But that's not McDonald's. McDonald's isn't real in the way that a chimpanzee or a banana is real. McDonald's is a story that millions of grown-ups tell each other and believe very strongly, but it exists only in our imagination. We created it with our special Sapiens superpower.

HOW STORIES
HELP

Maybe our ancestors once believed that there was a Great Lion Spirit who lived high above the clouds and who could help them find bananas, hunt giraffes, and catch fish. Well, in exactly the same way, grown-ups today

believe that there's a great spirit called McDonald's that can open restaurants, pay workers, and make lots of money.

Why did people invent such a weird story about a spirit called McDonald's? Because it's actually a very useful story. **For most of history, only real people could open restaurants,** pay workers, and make money. But that meant that if something went wrong, the person who owned the restaurant was in big trouble.

For example, what would happen if you borrowed money to open a restaurant, but nobody came to your restaurant and you couldn't pay back the money? You would have to sell your house, your shoes, and even your socks in order to pay back the money you borrowed. You might end up sleeping naked on the street! Also, if somebody ate in your restaurant and got very sick, you would be to blame, and you could end up in jail. So people were afraid to open restaurants, or to start all kinds of other businesses. **Why take such big risks?**

That's why some very imaginative people came

up with the story of corporations. If you want to open a restaurant but you don't want to risk losing your socks or going to jail, you create a corporation. And then **the corporation does everything and takes all the risks.**

The corporation borrows money from the bank, and if it can't repay the money, nobody can blame you for it, and nobody can take your house or your socks. After all, the bank gave the money to the corporation, not to you. And if somebody eats a burger and gets a really nasty stomachache, **nobody can hold you responsible.** You didn't make that burger—the corporation did.

If you create a corporation, it can help you with plenty of things besides restaurants. Say Tina's dad asks, "Who left muddy footprints all over the floor?" Tina could reply, **"It wasn't me.** It was the Tina Corporation." That would make life so much easier, right? **Well, that's exactly what grown-ups do.** Whenever you blame them for something serious—like polluting the world—they just say, "It wasn't me. It was the corporation."

If you're finding all this confusing, that's perfectly okay. The story of corporations like McDonald's is very complicated. Even most grown-ups get confused if you ask them to tell this story. Only people called lawyers can tell it right.

Do you know how the McDonald's Corporation was created in the first place? It wasn't created when Richard and Maurice McDonald laid the first brick of their first restaurant or fried their first burger. It wasn't created when the first customer walked in and paid them a dollar. No, it was created when a lawyer performed a bizarre ceremony and told everybody a story: **the story of the McDonald's Corporation.**

To tell the story properly, the lawyer first had to put on special ceremonial robes—also known as a suit. If you're going to tell people an important story, you need to look impressive. Then the lawyer opened a lot of old books written in a language that nobody except lawyers understands: **legalese.** (Legalese is similar to, and actually borrows a lot of words from, Latin. Even the word *legalese* itself comes from Latin.)

The lawyer searched through these old books for the exact words needed to create McDonald's, then wrote them down on a beautiful piece of paper so they wouldn't be forgotten. Then the lawyer held up the piece of paper and read the story out loud to a lot of people.

Of course, nobody could see the McDonald's Corporation, or hear it, or touch it, or smell it. But still, all the adults were convinced that the McDonald's Corporation really did exist because they heard the story that the lawyer told, and they all believed it.

That's how McDonald's was created. And that's how other corporations were created—Google and Facebook and Mercedes-Benz and Toyota. They're all stories that grown-ups believe. And because everybody believes these stories, a lot of people can cooperate.

THE POWER OF A
PIECE OF PAPER

Today, about 200,000 people work for the McDonald's Corporation, and it earns about $6 billion every year. That's a lot of money! And all the workers are pretty keen to do whatever McDonald's tells them to do because then the corporation gives them some of its money.

So what is this money that McDonald's and Google and all the other corporations give people? What is this money that everybody wants so much? Well, money is also just another imaginary story that grown-ups believe. Take a look at some money. Maybe a dollar bill, or a rupee, or a five-euro note. What is it? It's just a piece of paper. You can't eat it, or drink it, or wear it.

But then along come some great storytellers called bankers and politicians, and they're even more powerful than lawyers. Grown-ups have a lot of faith in bankers and politicians and will believe almost any story they tell. They tell stories like "This small piece of paper is worth ten bananas," and the grown-ups believe them. And as

long as everyone believes this story, that small piece of paper really is worth ten bananas. You can take that piece of paper to a store and give it to a complete stranger, and the stranger will give you real bananas, which you can actually eat.

Of course, you can use the piece of paper to buy other things too. You can buy coconuts, or books, or anything else you want. You can, for example, go to McDonald's and buy a burger.

This is something chimpanzees can't do. Chimps do give things to one another, like meat and bananas. **Chimps sometimes even trade favors.** One chimp might give another a nice scratch on the back, and the second chimp might then pick fleas and thorns from the first one's fur. You scratch my back, I'll scratch yours. But if one chimp gave a dollar bill to another chimp and expected to get a nice juicy banana in return, all the chimps would be completely baffled. Chimps don't believe in money, and they certainly don't believe in corporations.

So that's how stories make it possible for thousands of strangers to cooperate. Without the story of soccer, you wouldn't know the rules of the game. You could kick a ball around with other kids, but you couldn't play soccer. Without the stories of corporations and money, you couldn't go to McDonald's and buy a burger.

A TINY BUT
VERY POWERFUL
BOTTLE OF OIL

So one thing that our storytelling superpower gives us is the ability to cooperate in very large numbers. But that isn't all. Our superpower also allows us to change the way we cooperate, and to make these changes quickly. As we saw earlier, ants can also cooperate in large numbers, even though they don't invent stories. But ants almost never change their behavior. For thousands of years, all ants have been doing exactly the same things—like serving the queen ant. In contrast, humans can quickly change the way we behave by simply changing the stories we believe.

For example, for many years France was ruled by kings because people believed that a great god above the clouds had said that France must be ruled by a king and that all French people must do whatever the king commanded. Did a god really say that? Most likely not. This was just a made-up story. But as long as French people believed this story, they all obeyed their king. And the king enjoyed this very much.

But how did people know who should be king? Well, there was a story about that too, and it's a seriously strange one. According to this strange story, when the great god above the clouds chose one brave warrior to

be the first king of France, the god performed an amazing miracle to show people his choice.

He sent a dove down from heaven carrying a small glass bottle full of very special oil. Nobody really saw this happen, but a priest showed people a glass bottle and said it came from the sky, and people kind of believed it. And when they came to crown the new king, the priest first poured this sky oil on the king's head.

And from then onward, whenever one king died and people came to crown his son as the new king

of France, they dabbed some of the special oil on his head. No oil, no king. And the bottle of oil was kept in a safe place.

BOYS
ONLY

The story of the sky oil helped convince the French that their king was sent by the great god above the clouds. That's why whenever the king ordered people to give him food, they all gave him lots of food, and he would have a mountain of apples and baguettes and smelly cheeses, even though lots of his people were hungry. And when he told them to build him a palace, they built him a huge palace, even though many of them lived in small huts. And when he told them to go fight the armies of other kings, they took their swords and shields and went to fight, and many of them were killed in wars.

And if anybody didn't want to do what the king ordered, people said, "But he has sky oil on his head! We must obey him!"

There's one question you might be asking yourself. The glass bottle was very small and didn't contain much oil. So you would think that after crowning a few kings, there would be no more sky oil left. And remember: no oil, no king. How would they get more of that sky oil?

What would you do if you were the king's son and you needed that bottle to have oil in it so that you could become the new king? Do you have an idea? You do? Well, the kings of France probably had exactly the same idea.

Anyway, every time people came to crown a new king, they found that the small glass bottle had enough oil in it. And the French believed that this was another miracle: it proved that the great god above the clouds really liked the new king.

But one day the king's daughter said that she wanted to put the sky oil on her head and become ruler of France. Everybody laughed at her.

"You can't rule France," they said, "because the great god above the clouds doesn't like girls very much. The great god above the clouds is a boy, so he made boys much smarter and braver than girls. So a girl can't rule the kingdom of France. Only boys can."

And because people believed the story, they wouldn't let girls become rulers. In fact, they wouldn't let them do all sorts of things: girls couldn't be ship captains or judges, or even go to school.

The story of the sky oil was extremely important because it helped decide who would rule France and who would tell millions of people what to do. The people of France believed this story for a very long time, and for more than a thousand years France was ruled by oily kings.

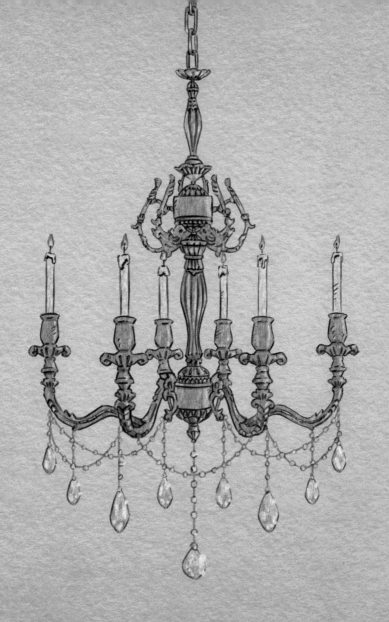

But in the end, some wise people started thinking about the story. "Hey, **this story's complete nonsense,**" one of them said. "Why does anyone believe it? No great god above the clouds says that France should be ruled by kings, or that boys are better than girls. The kings and their sons just invented the story so that people would do what they say."

"That's right," someone else agreed. "And why do people think that you need to put oil on your head in order to rule France? What a ridiculous idea! And does anyone really believe it was a miracle that that tiny bottle of oil never dried up? No way! Whenever they needed to crown a new king, a servant probably sneaked into the room where the oil bottle was kept and secretly poured ordinary kitchen oil into it!"

The people of France became very angry that they'd believed this nonsense for so many years and allowed all those kings to take their smelly cheeses and send them to fight nasty wars. So they captured the king and cut off his head. They found the old oil bottle and broke it to pieces . . . and no god from above the clouds came down to punish them. Historians call this time when the French stopped believing in kings the French Revolution.

Today, France no longer has a king. The people elect whomever they like to be president of France (and

you don't have to put oil on your head to be president). If after a few years people stop liking the president, they elect somebody else. And anybody can become president—girls as well as boys.

Of course, like people around the world, the French still believe in all kinds of other strange stories. The story of corporations, for example, and stories about complicated ideas like nationalism and democracy that we'll talk about another time. But there are two important things to remember: people need stories in order to cooperate, and they can change the way they cooperate by changing the stories they believe. That's why we're far more powerful than ants. That's our superpower.

A SQUAD OF
STORYTELLERS

So this is how our ancestors conquered the world: with stories. None of the other animals believe in stories. They only believe in things they can actually see, hear, smell, touch, or taste. A chimpanzee believes he's in danger when he sees a snake approaching—better run away! He believes there's a storm coming when he hears a clap of thunder—time for a shower! He believes there are lions nearby when he smells their poop—phooey! He believes fire is hot when he touches a burning branch—

ouch! And he believes bananas are tasty when he eats one—mmm, yummy!

We Sapiens can do all that too, of course, but because we believe in stories, we can do so much more. For example, when our ancestors spread across the world, whenever they encountered the Neanderthals, or the Floresians, or some very dangerous animal, a leader might have told them stories to encourage them. "The Great Lion Spirit wants us to get rid of the Neanderthals," the leader might have said. "The Neanderthals are very strong, but don't worry. Even if a Neanderthal kills you, that's actually a good thing because you'll go to the land of the spirits above the clouds, where the Great Lion Spirit will welcome you and give you lots of blueberries and giraffe steaks to eat."

And people believed the story, so they cooperated to get rid of the Neanderthals. Yes, the Neanderthals were very strong, but 50 Neanderthals were no match for 500 Sapiens all working together.

This belief in stories gave our ancestors so much power that they spread all over the world, conquering every land on the planet.

But what did they do after they conquered each new place and settled there? What was their life like thousands of years ago? They had plenty more things to figure out. What did they do when they woke up in the morning? What did they eat for breakfast—and lunch? What were their hobbies? Did they like to paint? What kind of

clothes and houses did they have? Did big brothers tease their little sisters? Did they fall in love? And was their life better or worse than ours?

In the next chapter, we'll try to answer questions like these and many more. We'll explain how our ancestors lived thousands of years ago, and how what they did then still affects what we love, what we fear, and what we believe today.

3

HOW OUR
ANCESTORS
LIVED

FOOD
MEMORIES

THOUSANDS OF YEARS AGO, OUR ANCESTORS LIVED very differently from us. But the way they lived has shaped how we behave today. When you're frightened of monsters in the night, that's a memory from your ancestors. Similarly, when you get up in the morning, eat breakfast, and play with friends, you often follow habits that were formed by our Stone Age ancestors in the savannahs of Africa.

For example, have you ever wondered why people want to eat things that are bad for their health, such as too much ice cream and chocolate cake? **Why does all the bad stuff taste so good?**

The answer is that our bodies think we're still living in the Stone Age, and back then it made perfect sense to binge on sweet and fatty food. Our ancestors didn't have supermarkets and refrigerators. When they were hungry, they walked through the woods and along rivers looking for something to eat. And they never came across an ice cream tree or a cola river! The only sweet food available then was ripe fruit or honey. When they found sweet fruit, the smart thing to do was to eat as much of it as possible as fast as possible.

Suppose a group of Stone Age gatherers went looking for food and came across a fig tree full of sweet ripe figs. Some gatherers ate only a few figs and then said, "That's enough for us. We're watching our figures." The other gatherers couldn't say anything because their mouths were so full of figs. They ate and ate and ate until they almost burst. The next day, everybody came back to the tree, but there were no figs left because a group of baboons had found the tree and eaten them all. The people who'd eaten lots of figs were still feeling a little full, but those who'd eaten just a few were now very hungry.

Archaeologists have found many statues from those times, and a lot of them are of full-figured women. The archaeologists named one particularly beautiful statue the Venus of Willendorf. (This wasn't her real name, of course. We don't know what people called her 30,000 years ago.) In Venus's day, body fat was a sign of health and success. Most people in the Stone Age didn't look like Venus, just as most people today don't look like the models in advertisements. But everybody knew they should eat as many sweet things as possible. It was good for you! A Stone Age parent might have scolded his child, saying, "Stop munching those floppy lettuce leaves right now and come eat your sweets!"

We've inherited this tendency to eat sweet things from our Stone Age ancestors. In the DNA instruction book inside our bodies, it says in big bold letters, "If you find something sweet, eat as much as possible as quickly as you can!"

Many things have changed since the days of the Venus of Willendorf. Most people these days don't have to walk across the savannah for hours looking for something to eat. Instead, when we're hungry, we take ten steps to the kitchen, open the refrigerator, and look inside. But when we see a chocolate cake in there, we still react in the same way Stone Age gatherers reacted to a fig tree.

Our body reads its instruction book and starts shouting, "Hey, we found something sweet! Wonderful! Let's gobble up all of it immediately! Hurry! If we wait, the baboons next door will eat it all first!" **The instruction book is outdated, but our bodies don't know** that we

now live in villages and cities rather than on the savannah. Our bodies don't know that there are such things as refrigerators and chocolate cake. Our bodies don't know that there are no baboons next door.

So we eat the whole chocolate cake, and the next day, we go to the supermarket and buy another cake. And when we open the refrigerator door, our body just can't believe its luck and starts shouting again, "Unbelievable! Something sweet! Eat it all up!" No matter how many times we open the refrigerator and find a chocolate cake there, our body doesn't learn. Again and again, it reacts as if we just discovered a fig tree in the savannah. It's very hard to remind ourselves that we're not in the Stone Age anymore, and that what made perfect sense in the days of our ancestors is no longer such a good idea.

That's why it's so important to find out how our ancestors lived. If we know how they lived, we can explain so much about how we behave today.

THE YOUNG
ARCHAEOLOGISTS

Unfortunately, there's a lot we don't know about the way our ancestors lived. We know they could sometimes cooperate in large numbers—this was their big advantage over Neanderthals, lions, and bears. But does this mean

they always lived together in large groups? For example, did 500 people live together in one very big cave? Or did every family live in a separate small cave and join the others only when they had something important to do together?

Did they live in caves at all?

Did they have families at all?

Let's start with the caves. Most people picture our Stone Age ancestors living in caves. This is because many of the things they left behind have been found in caves—things like stone tools, bones, and paintings on cave walls. Like the famous image of a wild horse painted 17,000 years ago in the Lascaux Cave in France.

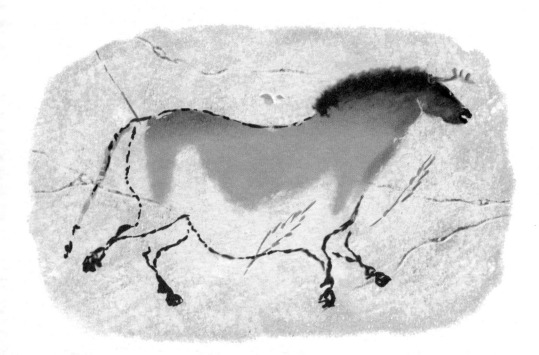

The Lascaux Cave wasn't discovered by professional archaeologists. It was found by four French teenagers who in 1940 went for a walk in the woods, came across a hole in the ground, and decided to investigate it. First, they threw stones into the hole to check how deep it was—they soon realized it led to a deep cave. So they climbed into the dark hole and down through a steep tunnel of wet clay into the unknown. They were quite brave! Their bravery paid off when they discovered a large chamber with hundreds of ancient paintings on the walls. It was one of the greatest archaeological discoveries of the twentieth century.

It wasn't the first time youngsters made such an amazing discovery. Around sixty years earlier, an archaeologist named Marcelino Sanz de Sautuola explored the Altamira Cave in Spain, and he brought along his eight-year-old daughter, Maria Justina, to keep him company. Marcelino busied himself poking around the bottom of the cave, carefully studying every tiny bump in the ground as he searched for ancient bones and stone tools. Maria thought this was boring, so she started looking up at the walls and ceiling. "Look, Daddy, bulls!" she cried. Marcelino looked up and saw wonderful paintings of bison and other animals all over the cave.

But finding many of their things in caves doesn't necessarily mean that ancient people usually lived in caves. In fact, they rarely did: they mostly camped in the open country, building wooden huts or making tents out of branches and animal skins.

NO PLACE LIKE
HOME

At Ohalo, on the shores of the Sea of Galilee in Israel, archaeologists found a good example of an ancient camp-site where people lived 23,000 years ago. There were six huts made of tree branches and straw, each with a camp-fire outside. It probably took just a few hours to build all these huts. The archaeologists also found various stone tools, some bones, and even a garbage dump with leftover food. **From the remains of this dump, we can tell what the people of Ohalo ate:** reptiles, birds, gazelles, deer, eight kinds of fish, lots of different fruits and vegetables, and other wild plants such as wheat, barley, and almonds.

The huts were lived in for a while but eventually burned down. Perhaps it was an accident, or perhaps the inhabitants had had enough of Ohalo and decided to move on. Luckily, shortly after they left, the whole site was flooded and covered with a thick layer of mud. When this mud hardened, it preserved everything just as it had been when the people left. That's how, all these years later, we know what the Ohalo camp looked like and what was in its garbage dump!

There were probably thousands of camps like Ohalo around the world, and most people lived in this sort of camp. But almost all the camps disappeared without a trace: the wood used to build them was destroyed by the wind and the rain, and their garbage was eaten by ants and jackals. Most things that have survived until today were left deep inside caves, where they were safe from jackals and rainstorms.

So, yes, people did occasionally visit caves, but they didn't live there all the time. They weren't cave people.

Imagine an asteroid from outer space hitting the earth sometime in the distant future and destroying all the buildings: every house, school, factory, and museum. The only things left would be the deepest subway tunnels. And the only human art left would be the graffiti, maps, and advertisements on subway station walls. If super-smart rats ruled the world one day, what would the rat scientists of the future think about us? Would they call us tunnel people?

STONE AGE
FAMILIES

What about families? What did families look like in the days of the Venus of Willendorf or the Ohalo campers? Was every hut in Ohalo home to one family? And what did *family* mean? Did it mean a man and a woman living together their entire lives and raising only their own children?

The truth is, we don't know for sure. Many people assume that humans always lived in families composed of a mother, a father, and the children they had together, but this is far from certain. Today, **there are many kinds of families in the world**—just take a look at your class.

Does everybody live with their mother and father? Probably not.

Nowadays, some people have one partner for their entire life, some have many partners, and some remain single. In a few countries, one man can be married to several women at the same time. In other countries, two women can get married to each other, and so can two men.

Some people have one child, some have ten, and some have none. **Some children are raised by a single mother or by a single father, or perhaps by their grandparents.** Others are adopted, and some have two fathers or two mothers. Sometimes parents separate and later find new partners, so a child might have a mother, a father, and also a stepfather and a stepmother. Some families include dozens of aunts, uncles, cousins, and

grandparents, all living together. So you might share a room with your cousin rather than your brother, and it might be your uncle or your grandmother who makes breakfast every day rather than your parents. There are so many options!

Our cousins the apes have a variety of different living arrangements too. Gibbons usually live in pairs: when a male gibbon and a female gibbon become a couple, they tend to stay together for many years. They live by themselves in their own part of the forest, taking care of their children.

With gorillas, it's much more common for one male to live with a lot of females and all their children. Every little gorilla has a different mother, but they all have the same father.

Orangutans like to be by themselves, enjoying peaceful solitude, perhaps just sitting in a tree watching the sunset. Orangutan mothers are almost always single moms, raising their young by themselves with no father around. And when the young grow up, they move out and go off to live alone. They don't feel sad about it—that's just the way they like it!

Chimpanzees are the exact opposite of orangutans: they live in big noisy communities of males and females. And unlike gibbons, they don't form permanent couples. Young chimps stay close to their mother, but they usually don't even know who their father is. In fact, they wouldn't understand what *father* means. In one kind of chimpanzee, the common chimpanzee, the males hang out together, and the most powerful male dominates the entire group. In another kind, called bonobos, the females form strong friendships, help one another raise the young, and tell the adult males what to do. Bonobo girls don't dream about marrying a handsome prince—they'd usually prefer a cool girlfriend!

Apes have many different kinds of families, and so do humans today. But what about humans in the Stone Age, like the people of Ohalo? When we look at the remains of the Ohalo huts, we can imagine different options.

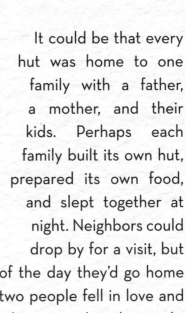

It could be that every hut was home to one family with a father, a mother, and their kids. Perhaps each family built its own hut, prepared its own food, and slept together at night. Neighbors could drop by for a visit, but at the end of the day they'd go home to their hut. If two people fell in love and decided to start living together, they might have a big marriage ceremony so that everybody knew about it, and then they would build a completely new hut just for themselves. **Maybe it was like that.**

Or maybe it was a little different. A man, a woman, and their three kids might have lived in one hut. In a neighboring hut, there could have been a woman with her two kids, plus her current boyfriend and his two kids. In the third hut, one woman and her child. In the fourth hut, one woman, her three children, and her current girlfriend. In the fifth hut, three old people living together with no kids. And in the sixth hut, one man living all by himself.

Or maybe it was totally different. Maybe there was no clear separation into families, and people lived in what is known as a commune. When the commune came to a new place and set up camp, everyone would work together, building several huts and tents, and they all slept and ate where they wanted. Perhaps on the first night you slept in one hut, but because somebody there snored very loudly, you'd move to another hut for the next night.

When you really liked somebody in the commune, you just moved your beds to the same hut, and that was it. There was no need to invite all your boring relatives for a big wedding party or go to the trouble of building a completely new hut and accumulating lots of stuff. When you no longer liked someone, you didn't have to hire expensive divorce lawyers to fight about who should get the hut and all the stuff and tell you where to sign on lots of important documents. You just took your bed and moved away. Actually, there might not even have been a bed to move because people slept on the ground.

If people did live in a commune like this, who took care of the children? Kids obviously knew who their mother was: she gave birth to them and took special care of them for years. But it's not clear whether Stone Age kids always knew who their father was. Perhaps all the men helped raise all the children by bringing them food, protecting them from lions, and teaching them how to climb trees and make stone knives. Maybe children could have close bonds with several adults in the commune, and nobody felt the need to define exactly who was a father, who was an uncle, and who was an unrelated neighbor.

This is similar to the arrangement our chimpanzee cousins have: they usually live in a kind of commune.

Well, maybe it was like that . . . and maybe not. It's easy to imagine different possibilities, but scientists need to distinguish imagination from fact. You can't say that something happened just because you imagined it: you need evidence. Evidence is something you don't have to imagine because you can actually see, touch, and taste it. Like the finger bone from the Denisova Cave. You can see that bone, you can touch it, and if you insist, you could even put it in your mouth and taste it . . . but it probably has a yucky old-bone taste.

STONE AGE
SELFIES

So what evidence do we have about how families actually looked in the Stone Age? Imagine some rat scientists thousands of years from now trying to understand what your family was like. How would they figure that out?

The rat scientists could look at your family's photo albums and know who was in the family, where you lived, and where you went on vacation. So wouldn't it be helpful if we found some photo albums from the Stone Age? Unfortunately, there were no cameras and no photo albums back then. We do have some cave paintings from that period—like the paintings in Lascaux and

Altamira—but most of them are of animals. There are no paintings of human families. And that's quite interesting, isn't it? Suppose you looked at somebody's photo album, and their pictures were all of horses, lions, and elephants. Not one photo of their family. What would that mean?

Maybe the Stone Age paintings are telling us that families weren't very important then.

Or maybe Stone Age people painted animals on stone walls in distant caves, but painted their own family on wooden boards that they could easily carry around and hang at the entrance to their hut. These were the really important pictures, so they wanted to have them nearby. Unfortunately, the wooden boards would have disappeared long ago. All that remains is the cave paintings of animals.

Maybe Stone Age people thought that when you painted something, you could control it. So everyone wanted to paint the animals they hunted to have control over them, but nobody ever wanted to have their own picture painted.

We don't really know, and there may be other explanations. Can you think of any?

The closest things we have to Stone Age family photos are the collections of handprints that people left on rocks and cave walls. How did people paint handprints on rocks when they didn't have spray cans? One important clue is that most of these handprints are of left hands, not right hands. Can you guess why?

Most people find it easier to use their right hand to operate tools. It seems that ancient people made these handprints using complicated spray tubes. This is what they probably did to make each handprint:

1. They crushed some colorful stones and mixed the powder with water to make liquid paint.
2. They poured the paint into a hollow tube made from straw, wood, or bone.
3. They placed their left hand on the wall while holding the tube carefully with their right hand.
4. They pointed one end of the tube at their left hand and blew into the other end.
5. The paint sprayed over their left hand. *Pshhhhhhht!*

When they took their left hand away, its outline remained on the wall. It would probably have been easier if somebody else sprayed the paint over their hand for them, but people apparently preferred to make their handprints all by themselves. These were the first selfies in history!

On some rocks archaeologists found just a single handprint. But in a few places there were lots of handprints grouped together. Each handprint was made by a different person, but they were probably all members of

the same group. Maybe this was the Stone Age way of doing a group selfie—everyone in the group came to the rock during some special festival and left their handprint there. You could try making a Stone Age group selfie like this at your next birthday party—and perhaps some rat scientists will find it in the future!

The problem is, we don't know how the ancient people who made these rock selfies were related to one another. Were they all brothers and sisters? Perhaps they were cousins? Or maybe just friends who came to celebrate somebody's birthday.

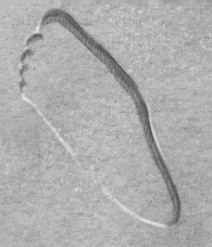

FOOTPRINTS
IN THE
SAND

We also have some footprints from the Stone Age. That sounds a bit unbelievable, right? Usually, if you leave a footprint on a sandy beach, it disappears within minutes. But in a place called Le Rozel on the Atlantic coast of France, archaeologists found no fewer than 257 footprints left by a group of people who walked over a sand dune 80,000 years ago. Luckily, the sand quickly hardened and turned into stone, which is why we can still see their footprints today.

The people who made these footprints were not Sapiens; they were Neanderthals. Having carefully examined each footprint, archaeologists concluded that they were left by a group of about twelve Neanderthals, most of them children and teenagers. One was just a toddler. This gives us a very important clue about

Neanderthal families—or about this particular Neanderthal group, at least.

They didn't live alone like orangutans, and they didn't live in small family units like gibbons. But we can't say much more than that about the dozen Neanderthals who walked on that sandy beach 80,000 years ago. Did they all have the same father? Did they all live together? Perhaps they were just a group of unrelated friends who met once a year to celebrate an important event on the beach. We can't be sure.

So we need more evidence. Those imaginary rat scientists in the future studying your family could look at all the stuff your family owns, and it would tell them a lot about how you live. How many chairs do you have in your house, how many beds, and how many computers? But Stone Age people didn't have a lot of stuff. In fact, that's the one thing we know for certain about our ancestors: no matter what kind of families they had, they managed to live with almost no stuff at all.

Today, a typical family owns several million things over the years. Think about the things you have: not just big things like chairs and computers, but also all the plastic bags, cereal boxes, candy wrappers, and toilet paper that you use every day. When you have a meal, you use cutlery and plates and glasses. When you play, you use balls and cards and game consoles. We usually don't notice how much stuff we have . . . until we move houses. Then we suddenly realize that we need lots and lots of boxes to pack up all our stuff. Some people have to hire a big truck and a couple of strong workers to help them move everything.

Our Stone Age ancestors moved very often. They rarely

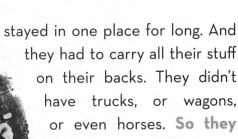

stayed in one place for long. And they had to carry all their stuff on their backs. They didn't have trucks, or wagons, or even horses. **So they didn't accumulate many things.** Instead of having lots of plates, cups, forks, and spoons, they ate with their hands, and if they needed to cut something, they could turn a stone into a knife.

However, people did have things besides stone knives. They had clothes made from animal skins, furs, and even feathers. They had wooden spears and clubs. They sometimes had huts made of tree branches and straw. But unfortunately, almost all these things rotted and disappeared long ago. **The only things that didn't rot were bones, teeth, and—especially—stones.** Stones never rot. They can last for millions of years.

A WORLD OF
STONE?

So, almost all the evidence we have from the Stone Age is made of stone . . . and that's why we call it the Stone Age. **But this is actually a very misleading name.** When people hear the words "Stone Age," they imagine that everything back then was made of stone: they think that people had stone beds, stone hats, and stone shoes. The truth is that most things were made of wood, straw, animal hide, and feathers. But these things disappeared long ago, and all that's left is the stones. This is why it's so difficult to know for sure how our ancestors lived in the Stone Age.

Fortunately, there is one other way that we can find out about how our ancestors lived: by watching living people. **There are a few places in the world where people still live a little like our ancestors did.** If we visit them, we can learn a lot.

In general, people can be divided into three groups: people who grow their food, people who buy their food, and people who hunt and gather their food. The people who grow their food are farmers. They might grow wheat to make bread, and plant apple trees so they can eat apples. Perhaps they keep chickens and eat their eggs, and sometimes they eat the chickens too.

Most people today don't grow their food—they buy it. When they're hungry, they go to the market and buy

bread and apples and eggs. Or they take out their smart-phone and order pizza.

Our Stone Age ancestors didn't grow their food or buy it: they hunted and gathered. This is what all animals do. Giraffes don't plant trees, and lions don't buy giraffe steaks at the supermarket. Giraffes feed on trees that naturally grow in the savannah, and lions hunt giraffes. **Similarly, our ancestors gathered wild plants and hunted wild animals.** This is why our ancestors are often called hunter-gatherers—or just gatherers—because they gathered their food from the wild.

Today, there are a few groups of people around the world who still hunt and gather their food. They don't live in houses and cities, and they don't work in factories or offices. **They mostly live in remote jungles and deserts.** Scientists can visit these people and see how they live, and by studying their lifestyle, the scientists can try to learn how our ancestors lived many thousands of years ago.

Of course, **being a gatherer today isn't the same as in the Stone Age.** Even gatherers who live in the most remote deserts and jungles are part of the modern world. If you see a gatherer child spreading her arms wide, running in circles, and making a noise like an air-plane engine, that doesn't mean people in the Stone Age had airplanes. It only means that modern-day gatherers must have seen airplanes flying across the sky. All the same, observing modern gatherers does give us a few more clues about what life was like in the Stone Age.

WHAT HAPPENS
AFTER YOU DIE?

So, using both archaeological evidence and observation of modern gatherers, what can we say about the way people lived in the Stone Age?

The most important thing to know is that there wasn't just one way of living but many different ways— not everybody did the same things. The world was home to thousands of different tribes, each with a different language, a different culture, different kinds of families, and a different way of life.

One reason for all the differences was that people lived in a wide variety of places, so they had to adapt to all sorts of ecosystems and climates. People who lived near a river ate a lot of fish and learned to build boats, while people who lived high in the mountains didn't even know how to swim. People who lived in tropical forests walked around almost completely naked, while people who lived in the Arctic dressed in heavy fur coats.

But even tribes that lived side by side may have had very different ways of life because they told different stories about the world. Remember, storytelling was the great advantage that Sapiens had over other animals. Whereas all bees in all beehives behave more or less the same, every human tribe was different because each tribe believed different stories.

For example, one tribe might have believed that after you died, you came back as a new baby, or perhaps even as an animal. Maybe a second tribe believed that when you died, you became a ghost. A third tribe may have thought that these two theories were a load of nonsense—when you died, you were gone, and that was that.

Perhaps in one tribe everybody lived together in a single big group, but in a nearby tribe people kept to their own small family. In one tribe it could have been perfectly acceptable for a man to marry another man, but not okay for one person to marry several people. In another tribe, a man might have been allowed to marry two or even ten women, but not another man. And maybe in a third tribe, people didn't even know what marriage meant: if you liked somebody, the two of you just lived together without making a big deal out of it.

There would also have been differences in things like art and the way people interacted. One tribe might have made beautiful cave paintings, whereas a neighboring tribe might have preferred dancing and singing instead. Maybe one tribe was very violent and its people were always fighting, but another could have been peaceful, its people friendly to everyone.

Attitudes toward Neanderthals and other kinds of humans might have varied too. Perhaps in one tribe

children were taught to fear or hate Neanderthals and told, "If you meet a Neanderthal kid in the forest, run away as fast as you can!" Maybe a second tribe had better relations with the neighboring Neanderthals, and if they really, really wanted to, they could play with the Neanderthal kids. And in a third tribe, perhaps they could even marry a Neanderthal, and nobody would think there was anything wrong with that.

While every gatherer tribe had its own special way of seeing the world and handling life, a few things were still common to people all over the world. In particular, people everywhere could cooperate in large numbers.

A small campsite like Ohalo would have been home to just one human band of about twenty to forty people. But this band probably belonged to a larger tribe made up of several bands. There could have been hundreds of people in the tribe as a whole. Everybody in the tribe

spoke the same language, believed the same stories, and followed the same rules. A tribe like that was different from a modern country: it had no government, no army, no police force. **But belonging to a large tribe had many advantages.**

Let's say, for example, that one band up in the mountains had good stones for making sharp knives—it could share them with the Ohalo band on the shores of the lake. In return, the Ohalo band could supply the mountain band with seashells and fish. If a woman in the Ohalo band invented a new way to make fishing nets, she could show people in other bands around the lake how to do it. If the fish in the lake became sick and died one year, all the lake bands could go live with the mountain bands for a while. And if another year there was a drought and all the mountain springs dried up, the mountain bands could go live with their cousins by the lake. So belonging to a tribe meant that people had sharper knives, better fishing nets, and more food in hard times.

250
FOX TEETH

You might wonder how we know that tribes existed at all. **Do we have any evidence** that hundreds of people spread over a wide area sometimes cooperated with one another? Well, yes, we do, and here's an example of this evidence: archaeologists studying Stone Age camps hundreds of miles from the sea quite often find seashells. How did these seashells get there? Most likely, bands that lived inland got them from bands that lived near the sea.

Another important piece of evidence was found in a place called Sunghir, in Russia, where archaeologists discovered a graveyard from 34,000 years ago. Some of the graves contained only a human skeleton . . . but in one grave they found the skeleton of a forty-year-old man covered with 3,000 beads made from mammoth ivory. The man had twenty-five ivory bracelets on his wrists and a hat decorated with fox teeth on his head. The hat was probably made of leather or fur, so it didn't survive, but the fox teeth were still there.

Then the archaeologists found an even more interesting grave. It contained several beautiful works of art and the skeletons of two boys who had been buried head to head. One boy was nine years old, and the other twelve. Both were wearing lots of ivory bracelets. The younger boy was covered with around 5,400 ivory beads, the older boy with about 5,000. He also had a fox-tooth hat and a belt decorated with 250 fox teeth. We're guessing fox teeth were the height of fashion in Stone Age Sunghir!

How can we explain this? Why did some graves contain so many valuable objects, while others had nothing but a skeleton? The easiest explanation is that the forty-year-old man was an important tribal leader, and perhaps the boys were his children or grandchildren, so they got a special burial too. This is what scientists thought for a long time. But when they finally succeeded in reading the DNA instruction book for these three skeletons, it turned out that the boys weren't brothers or even cousins, and the man wasn't their father or grandfather.

So **maybe there's another explanation.** Perhaps the members of the tribe believed a strange story, and they sacrificed a man and two children to please some great spirit above the clouds. Maybe they believed that if they sacrificed these three people to the spirit, the spirit would send them a lot of mammoths to hunt. We don't know for sure, but one thing is clear: hundreds of people had to work together to make all the valuable objects found in the graves with those three skeletons.

Let's take a closer look at the belt worn by the older boy. It was made using 250 fox teeth, but not any old tooth would do! No, they had to be the long, sharp canine teeth. Foxes have only four canine teeth—or fewer if they lose one somehow. Now do the math: How many foxes would you need to hunt in order to make a belt like that? Well, quite a lot: to get 250 fox canines, you would have to hunt at least sixty-three foxes and pull out their teeth. **That's an awful lot of work!** Foxes are very smart animals, and it could take a day or two to hunt just one fox. So it would have taken more than two months to get those teeth.

And what about the mammoth-ivory beads? To make them, you first had to hunt a mammoth, which is even harder than hunting a fox. A mammoth could reach a height of thirteen feet and weigh up to twelve tons—that's about the weight of a typical school bus. So you couldn't possibly hunt a mammoth by yourself; you needed a whole group of people to do it.

And after you hunted a mammoth, you then had to carve the tusks to make ivory beads. It would have taken a skilled artist about forty-five minutes to make a single bead. Now, the nine-year-old boy had around 5,400 of these beads, the older boy had 5,000, and the man had 3,000. **It would have taken 10,000 hours of hard work** to make all those beads. If you worked on it six hours a day and you didn't take a single day of rest, it would take you four and a half years to make that many beads.

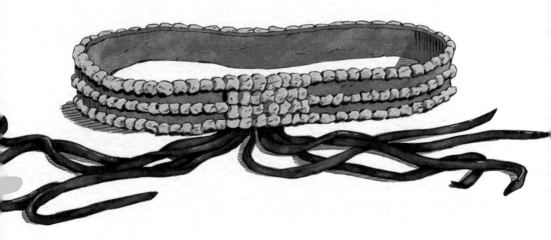

It seems very unlikely that just ten or twenty people could have made all the things in the Sunghir graves by themselves. **It was probably the work of hundreds of people.** The Sunghir graves are one of the best pieces of evidence we have that 34,000 years ago at least some people already belonged to big tribes.

BANDING
TOGETHER

Even though people belonged to big tribes, we know that they didn't live with the entire tribe all the time. It was difficult to find enough food for such a large group, so tribes split into smaller bands and went to different places to look for food. This meant that each tribe was made up of several smaller bands; one band could have had 100 people in it, another only ten.

People probably lived in their own small band most of the time, going from place to place in search of food. All the bands from one tribe came together only on special occasions: for instance, if an important person died, everybody would come to the funeral. They might also join forces when they wanted to hunt big animals, fight powerful enemies, or celebrate a major event. But most people lived for many months without meeting any human being from outside their small band.

Everybody within the band knew everybody else very well. **You were always surrounded by family and friends, and you did most things together.** You went to the forest to look for food together, you cooked and ate together, and you told stories around the campfire together. Some people might think this sounds wonderful. Others might not like the idea of never being alone and always seeing the same people. But when you got tired of the people in your band, you could usually move to another one. **That's how things still work in gatherer tribes today.** And if you went to a tribal event and became best buddies with somebody from another band, they could come live in yours—or you could go live in theirs.

The band didn't have one powerful leader who told everyone what to do. When decisions needed to be made—like which way to go or where to set up camp—everybody could say what they thought. If some big shot started bullying everyone and telling the band to make more and more fox-tooth hats for him, people could simply walk away and leave the bully behind. Today, when someone becomes a dictator, it's very difficult for people to leave their country. But in the Stone Age, people could usually vote with their feet.

THE GREAT
GATHERERS

What else can we learn about Stone Age life from archae-ology and from observing present-day hunter-gatherers? Today, hunter-gatherer bands don't stay in one place the whole time, and Stone Age bands probably also moved around in search of food. When there were fish in the river, they went to the river to catch fish. When figs were in season, they went to the forest to look for figs. They usually traveled back and forth across the territory that was their home. Home didn't mean a stone structure or a village; it meant a wide area full of mountains and forests and rivers.

How long does it take you to get from one end of your home to the other? For most people, it takes less than a minute. Even if you live in a giant palace, it still wouldn't take more than five minutes. But for our ancestors in the Stone Age, it could have taken about a week to walk from one side of their home to the other.

Sometimes there was so much food in a particular place that one or more bands could settle there for several months, or even the whole year. This happened most often near lakes and rivers full of fish and oysters, and with lots of birds around. People might have built a permanent village somewhere like that.

On other occasions, there wasn't enough food for everyone in the band, so it split. Some people stayed in the old home, and others left, walking until they found a new home. There were even occasions when an entire band abandoned its home territory. This might happen because of some natural disaster. Perhaps there was a long drought, the river dried up, the trees died, and there was nothing to eat. The band would have to travel a long way to find food. And that's how our ancestors gradually spread all over the world.

Gathering was a very interesting way of life, and every day people did different things. People gathered many kinds of plants, caught all sorts of tasty worms and insects, and also collected stones, wood, and bamboo in order to make tools and huts. Occasionally, they hunted big animals like mammoths and bison. This was difficult and dangerous, and required many people to work together, so it was kept for special occasions. But even a couple of kids rummaging around in the forest for an hour could always find a few wild carrots or onions. They could climb a tree to steal eggs from a bird's nest, or cut down bamboo to make a fishing rod.

Most of the time our ancestors were gatherers rather than hunters. And they didn't just gather food, stones, and wood—they also gathered knowledge. They didn't go to school or read books, but they were always learning. They couldn't survive without learning about all kinds of stuff.

First, they needed to get to know their territory. If they didn't

know where to find water, they would go thirsty. If they didn't know where to find food, they would go hungry. If they didn't know how to walk in a dark forest, they might fall down and break a leg. Gatherers walked through the same forests and over the same hills again and again, and eventually they were familiar with every spring, every tree, and every rock—**these things became like old friends.** You can find the bathroom, the refrigerator, and the cutlery drawer even in the middle of the night, can't you? Well, gatherers could find the refreshing spring, the big walnut tree, and the hill with the sharp flint stones even in the dark.

Gatherers also knew the plants and animals around them. They knew where mushrooms liked to grow, and they could tell the difference between a tasty mushroom

that could feed you, a poisonous mushroom that could kill you, and a medicinal mushroom that could cure an illness. They knew the season when birds laid their eggs, and they knew where each type of bird liked to nest. They knew where bears liked to hang out, and they knew what to do if a big bear started running after them.

Gatherers were also experts at making things. When we need a knife, a pair of shoes, or some medicine, we go to the store and buy it. We usually have no idea who made it and how. Maybe it came from the other side of the world. In the Stone Age, everybody needed to make their own stuff. If you wanted a knife, you first had to know where to find good flint stones. You had to go there and start your search, picking up and checking out a lot of stones. You examined each one carefully, looking at its shape and feeling its weight and texture. When you finally found a good stone, you hammered away at it with another rock or with a piece of wood, chipping off flakes of stone to sharpen the edge . . . but you had to be very careful not to break it. When modern people try to do this, they usually break dozens of stones and perhaps

a finger or two before they succeed, and it takes them hours, if not days, to produce a knife. **Gatherers could turn a flint stone into a sharp knife within minutes.** This is because they practiced from early childhood.

Archaeologists studying the remains of ancient camp-fires made some interesting discoveries. Close to where the fire had been, they found lots of stone chippings but only a few broken stones. In contrast, farther away from the fire, there were still many stone chippings but also plenty of broken stones. Why do you think that was?

It seems that the adults sat close to the fire: they were already experts at making knives and rarely broke a stone by mistake. Meanwhile, the children sat farther away, and they were still learning this art, so they broke lots of stones before they got it right.

So the gatherers learned about the animals, plants, and stones around them. But they also learned a lot about their own bodies, and how to use them. **They could listen, look, and move much better than we can.** When they walked in the forest, they listened for the slightest movement in the undergrowth—perhaps a snake was slithering past. *Tssssss.*

They looked closely at the nearby trees and could spot fruit, beehives, and birds' nests hidden in the leaves. They sniffed the air and could tell by the smell of it if a tiger was approaching or a deer was escaping. If a gatherer put a berry in her mouth, she con-centrated on how it tasted—a slightly soapy flavor

could mean the difference between a poisonous berry and one that was safe to eat. When bands went looking for stones, they ran their fingers over each one, carefully feeling the texture—**every stone spoke to them in the language of touch.** Smooth or rough? Soft or hard? That's how they knew which stone might break too easily and which would make a good knife.

When they walked, they made very little noise so as not to attract predators. When they ran, they were very fast, even on the most difficult terrain, jumping over rocks and logs and avoiding trees and thorny bushes. When they sat, they could stay in the same position for a long, long time, not moving a finger or scratching their nose but just watching and listening attentively.

In other words, **gatherers knew a whole lot!** We usually think that people today know far more than people did in ancient times. Of course, society as a whole knows more—we know how to build cars and computers and spaceships—but each individual actually knows less. Can you build a car? Or a computer? Or a spaceship? Even in factories where these things are made, each person usually knows how to do just one tiny thing. One person knows how to operate the machine that produces car tires, but that person doesn't know how to make the engine, the steering wheel, or the headlights.

It's the same in all professions. What do you need to know in order to fly an airplane or write a history book like this one? You need to know plenty about one thing,

but **for everything else, you rely on other people's help** . . . and each of those people also knows a lot about only one thing. People who write history books know a great deal about history, which is why they're called historians. But they may not know how to produce all their own food or sew their clothes or construct their houses. They write books, and people buy these books, and that's how historians earn money. Then the historians give some of their money to other people when they buy food, clothes, and a place to live. If you dropped a historian alone in the jungle, there's a chance he'd starve or be eaten by a tiger because writing a history book won't keep you alive in the jungle.

THE GOOD
OLD DAYS

In the Stone Age, gatherers who knew enough about the surrounding world often lived good lives. **They actually worked far less than many people do today.**

Let's think about a typical day for a factory worker in our time. She leaves home around seven in the morning and travels in a crowded bus through streets full of pollution to a big noisy factory. There she operates a machine for ten hours, doing the same thing over and over, then takes the bus back and gets home at seven in the evening.

And now she probably has to make a meal for her family, wash the dishes, do the laundry, clean the floor, and pay the bills.

Twenty thousand years ago, a gatherer might leave camp with her friends at eight in the morning. They'd walk through nearby forests and meadows, collect berries, climb trees to pick fruit, dig roots from the ground, catch a few fish, and sometimes run away from tigers. By about noon they'd be back at camp to make lunch. That's it. **That was the entire workday.** A good gatherer could usually find enough food within three or four hours to feed herself and her family for the whole day. And after lunch, there were no dishes to wash, no laundry to do, no floors to clean, and no bills to pay. That left plenty of time for gossiping, telling stories, playing with the children, and just hanging out with friends. Of course, tigers sometimes caught and

ate gatherers, or a snake bit them, but they didn't have to deal with car accidents or industrial pollution.

Gatherers usually ate better, more varied food than many modern factory workers, and they suffered less from starvation and disease. Archaeologists who examined the skeletons of gatherers discovered that they were quite strong and healthy because they ate a lot of different things. One day, they could eat berries and mushrooms for breakfast, then fruits, snails, and a turtle for lunch, and grilled rabbit with wild onions for dinner. The following day, they might have fish for breakfast, nuts and eggs for lunch, and an entire tree full of figs for dinner. Because they ate so many different things, they usually got all the vitamins and minerals they needed. If the nuts didn't contain some important vitamin, surely the mushrooms or snails did.

Also, because they didn't depend on just one kind of food, gatherers seldom starved. When people later switched to farming, they usually focused on growing one type of crop. Have you ever seen a wheat field, a potato field, or a rice field? In a wheat field there's nothing but wheat, a potato field has only potatoes, and in a rice field it's rice, rice, and rice. This made it easy for farmers to look after their fields, but it also meant that they had a very limited diet. If they grew only rice, then they had to eat rice for breakfast, rice for lunch, and rice for dinner too. And if a disease came along and killed the rice plants, they'd have nothing to eat. Disasters like that were quite common, so farmers were always in danger of starvation.

Gatherers were much safer. If a disease destroyed all the wild onions or killed all the rabbits in one area, gatherers had a tough time, but there were usually other things they could gather or hunt. No grilled rabbit in wild onion sauce this year? That's a shame, but we can pick more berries and catch more fish instead!

Gatherers were healthy not only because they ate so many different things, but also because there were fewer infectious diseases back then. Most of the infectious diseases we know today—like smallpox, measles, and flu—came to us from animals. Flu comes from chickens, ducks, and other birds. Measles, tuberculosis, and anthrax originally jumped to humans from cows, goats, and other farm animals. The COVID-19 pandemic may have started with bats. And because today we live in crowded villages and big cities, if even a single person catches a new virus from a chicken or a bat, it can quickly spread to thousands of other people.

Ancient gatherers had much less contact with animals. True, they hunted animals, but they didn't farm them or sell them in markets. Nobody had a chicken coop or a goat herd. Also, gatherers lived in small groups that moved around a lot. So even if someone caught a new disease from an animal, that sick person wouldn't have infected many other people.

So, was the Stone Age the best time ever? If you had a time machine and could travel wherever you wanted, should you set the destination to the Stone Age? Some people would. They dream about the days when we roamed freely over woods and meadows, when "school" meant playing with bows and arrows and "work" meant hiking in the forest. But before you press the button and join a band of Stone Age gatherers, we should take a look at the downsides of their life so that you know what you're getting into. And there sure were some downsides!

THE BAD
OLD DAYS

Let's start with the small stuff, like insects—Stone Age people were often bothered by insects. That doesn't sound like a big deal, but you could try a little test yourself. If it's warm enough, go outside, find somewhere nice and safe to lie down—perhaps under a tree—and try not to move at all for a whole hour. You're not allowed to move so much as a finger or to scratch your ear. Just wait. You won't have to wait very long: brave ants will soon be crawling up your feet, a mosquito might start buzzing around your ear, and an annoying fly might settle on your nose. And as for the spiders—ah, but don't move! Just keep lying there. After an hour, ask yourself if you really want to go back to a time when you always had to sleep under a tree or in a makeshift hut with all the insects. Remember that there were no houses where you could shelter behind solid walls and beneath a roof.

And of course, it wasn't just the insects—people constantly had to worry about lions, snakes, and crocodiles too. If you watch tigers on TV or even if you see live tigers

in the zoo, you feel safe because they can't come at you out of the TV or escape from their cage. But what if the tigers were out, prowling around your neighborhood? Would you feel safe leaving the house to walk to school or meet a friend?

And then there was the weather. When it rained, the gatherers got wet. Soaking wet. They were cold in winter and hot in summer. And they couldn't just hide in a deep cave all day. If they didn't go to look for food, or if they didn't find any food, they went hungry.

Sadly, accidents were quite common, and because gatherers had no hospitals or modern medicines, even a minor injury could be very dangerous. Say a boy climbing a tree to pick some fruit fell and broke his leg; he couldn't just stay in bed for a month. And anyway, there weren't any beds. The other people in the band would

help him as much as they could, but if he couldn't keep up when they moved to a new camp, or if he couldn't run away from lions, he was in serious trouble.

Children in particular faced many dangers. They needed lots of food to grow big and strong, and they weren't yet experts in climbing trees and dealing with dangerous animals. There were new tests every day: On Monday, you might have your watching-out-for-snakes test. On Tuesday, a test in finding your way in a dark forest, and then mammoth hunting on Wednesday. On Thursday, it could be swimming across an icy river, and on Friday, telling the difference between safe mushrooms and poisonous ones. And there was no weekend break—on Saturday, you could be tested in tree climbing, and on Sunday, on stealing honey without being stung by hundreds of bees.

If you failed one of these tests, you didn't just get a bad grade—you could die. Maybe our world isn't so terrible, after all!

TALKING TO THE
ANIMALS

If you watch cartoons or read fairy tales, you're very likely to come across trees and animals that talk. Little children happily believe that we can talk to trees and animals. They also accept the idea that there are ghosts and spirits around us, spying on what we do or hiding in the attic.

Grown-ups think this is adorable and funny. As children grow up, they're told that there are no ghosts or talking trees, and only little kids believe in all that.

But it seems that in the Stone Age, adults also believed that trees and animals could talk and that ghosts and spirits existed. When they walked through forests, gatherers talked to bushes and stones and asked for help from elephants and mice. They listened closely to what the birds said. If somebody fell sick or there was an accident, they might well blame a ghost or ask a spirit for advice.

How do we know this? Well, we don't know it for sure, of course. It's usually easier to know what people do than what they think. For example, we know for sure that people in Sunghir hunted mammoths because we've found lots of mammoth bones there. But what did the people of Sunghir think about mammoths? Were some of them vegetarians who thought it was wrong to kill animals? And if an angry mammoth trampled on a person and killed him, what did they think happened to that person? Did they believe that dead people went to heaven, or were reborn into a new body, or became ghosts . . . or just vanished into the dark?

It's very hard to answer these questions because we can't ask Stone Age people. Today, if you want to know what Muslims believe, you can simply ask a Muslim or read the Qur'an. If you want to know what Christians believe, you ask a Christian or read the Bible. If you want to know what Hindus believe, you ask a Hindu or read the Vedas.

Stone Age people weren't Muslims, Christians, or Hindus: they couldn't be because these religions appeared only in the last 3,000 years. The Qur'an was composed about 1,500 years ago, the Bible about 2,000 years ago, and the Vedas maybe 2,500 years ago.

People who lived 20,000 years ago didn't read or write, so we don't have any holy books from the Stone Age. We do get a few hints about their beliefs from graves like the ones at Sunghir, from statues like the Stadel lion-man, and from cave paintings like the ones that the teenage archaeologists found in the Lascaux Cave. It's interesting that there are lots of animals painted in Lascaux but no gods—at least, there's nothing that looks like a god to us. So maybe they didn't believe in powerful gods.

But remember those modern gatherers who live in remote corners of the world today? A good way to research what Stone Age gatherers might have believed is to talk to modern gatherers. And sure enough, many of these gatherers don't believe in powerful gods, but they do believe that animals, trees, and even rocks can talk, and that the world is full of ghosts and spirits. So scientists

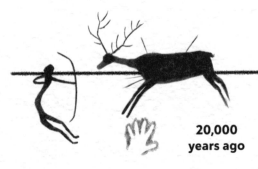

20,000 years ago

have concluded that in hunter-gatherer societies—today and in the Stone Age—both adults and children often believe you can talk with trees and animals.

One example of modern gatherers is the Nayaka people, who live in the jungles of southern India. When a Nayaka comes across a dangerous animal such as a tiger, snake, or elephant in the jungle, the Nayaka might talk directly to the animal: "You live in the forest, and I live in the forest too. You came here to eat, and I came here to gather roots and tubers. I didn't come to hurt you, so please don't hurt me."

A Nayaka was once killed by a male elephant they called "the elephant who always walks alone." People from the Indian government then came to capture the elephant, but the Nayaka refused to help the government officials. They explained that the elephant had a good reason to be violent: he used to have a very close friend, another male elephant, and the two always roamed the forest together. One day, some bad people shot the second elephant and took him away. "The elephant who always walks alone" had been very lonely ever since and was very angry at humans. "How would you feel if your

2,500 years ago   **2,000 years ago**   **1,500 years ago**

partner was taken away from you?" the Nayaka asked. "That's exactly how this elephant felt. The two elephants sometimes went their separate ways at night, but in the morning, they always came together again. On that terrible day, the elephant watched his buddy fall to the ground. If two creatures are always together and then you shoot one, **how's the other one going to feel?"**

Scientists have invented a special word for people who believe that animals can talk and that there are spirits who live in rocks and rivers: animists. Do you know where the word *animist* comes from? That's right, Latin. In Latin, the word *anima* means "spirit." A spirit is something that can feel things and want things and talk with other spirits about what it feels and wants. For animists, **it makes perfect sense to talk to trees, elephants, flowers, or stones** because animists think that all these things have spirits.

For example, animists might believe that the big walnut tree at the top of a hill has a spirit. The tree enjoys the rain and the sun, and gets upset if people cut off her branches to make spears. When the tree's happy, she

grows plenty of walnuts
and shares them with humans, squirrels,
and crows. When she's angry, she stops growing walnuts,
and to make matters worse, she can make people sick.
How does she do that? Well, the tree spirit has many
friends because she allows all kinds of smaller spirits and
ghosts to live among her branches. So if a man makes the
tree spirit angry, she asks some of these smaller spirits to
fly into the man's nose or mouth, make their way down
his throat and into his stomach, and give him a terrible
stomachache.

Sure, the tree can talk with all these little spirits, but
she can also talk directly to people. And people can talk
right back. The man who angered the tree and became
sick could ask the tree for forgiveness. If he was lucky,
**the tree might forgive him and ask the little spirits to
come back out of his stomach.**

Of course, talking to a tree isn't easy. First, you need
to learn the tree's language, and that takes time and
patience. We all know you can't learn Chinese or Swedish

in a day, and this is the same: you can't learn the language of trees, stones, or frogs in a day. Treebrish, Stonish, and Froggish are complicated languages. They aren't made of words. **They're made of signs, sounds, movements, and even dreams.** Most people today can't talk with trees, but animists would say that this isn't because trees don't talk—no, it's because people have forgotten the language of trees.

Most people today think that we humans are the most important things in the world, but animists believe that all spirits are equal. Humans are no more important than trees, and mammoths are no more important than frogs. Everybody has a place in the world, and nobody has total power. Animists don't give much importance to big gods. The spirits they talk with are small, local ones. If you want something from the walnut tree at the top of the hill, you have to talk with that particular tree, not the goddess of all trees or the great god of the sky. And that makes sense. It's like when you want your sister to share her chocolate bar with you: you have to talk to your sister, not the goddess of sisters!

For animists, **the rules that govern the world aren't dictated by one great god. Instead, they are decided by all the spirits in the world discussing them together.** Humans talk with trees and wolves and all the other spirits to decide how everybody should behave.

PLAYING BY THE
RULES

What sort of rules did the gatherers have? Well, the rules weren't the same everywhere, because they weren't decided by a single great god in the sky. In every area, there were different animals, trees, and stones, so people believed in different rules. The rules in Sunghir were different from those in Ohalo, which were different from those in Lascaux and Stadel. We can find out about the Nayaka people's rules today because we can talk to the Nayaka and ask them. But we can't know exactly what rules the ancient people of Sunghir, Ohalo, Lascaux, and Stadel followed because we don't have enough evidence. And the evidence we do have can be interpreted in many ways.

Take a look at the painting below, for example. Gatherers painted it in the Lascaux Cave about 17,000 years ago. What do you think it's about?

Many people would agree that it's an image of a man with a head like a bird with a bison next to him and a bird underneath him. Okay, but what does it mean? Well, some archaeologists say that the bison has attacked the man, and that the man is falling down dead. They say that the bird underneath the man represents his spirit flying away at the moment of death. And maybe the big scary bison isn't just an ordinary animal but a symbol of death itself. So, these archaeologists claim that this painting is proof that some people 17,000 years ago believed that

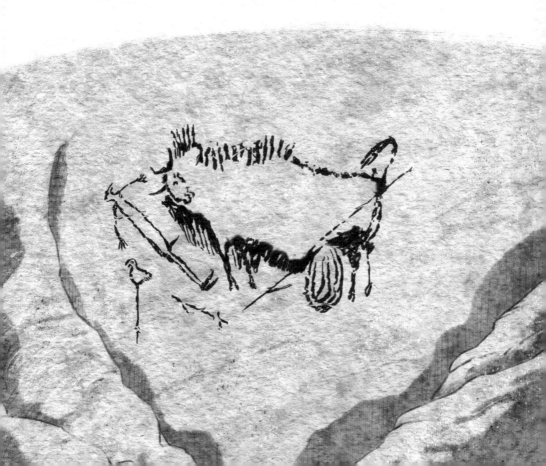

when they died, their spirits would be freed from their bodies and fly away to heaven, or perhaps enter a new body. Well, *maybe* that's what they believed.

And maybe not. **We have no way of knowing whether this theory is true.** Perhaps what some people see as a man with a bird's head is just a clumsy painting by someone who wasn't very good at drawing heads. After all, the man's hands and feet don't look very convincing either. And even if the head really is a bird's head, maybe this is a picture of a Stone Age Batman or Superman fighting an evil bison monster and flying away just when the bison's about to attack.

Or, if you look at it another way, maybe the man isn't falling down dead at all. He could be spreading his arms wide to hug the bison, and the bison's lowering his head to cuddle the man. So the image could be about the friendship between people and bison, right? If you stare at the painting for a while and let your imagination run free, you will likely come up with plenty more equally possible stories.

When we don't know something, it's best to be honest about it. We don't know exactly what people believed in the Stone Age, or what kind of stories they told. **It's one of the biggest gaps in our understanding of human history.**

So far, we've talked about how gatherers lived in general. But the important things in people's lives aren't the "in general" bits. History is made of specific events, and most history books describe these events in great detail.

THE CURTAIN OF
SILENCE

For instance, a history book about the first moon landing might describe how on July 20, 1969, at exactly 17 minutes and 43 seconds past 8 p.m., the spacecraft *Eagle* touched the surface of the moon at a place named Tranquility Base. It had two men on board: Neil Armstrong and Buzz Aldrin. (A third astronaut, Michael Collins, waited for them on board the mother ship, *Columbia*.) Armstrong then called NASA's mission control back on Earth, in the city of Houston, and said, "Houston, Tranquility Base here. **The *Eagle* has landed.**" At least 600 million people all over the world sat glued to their TVs and radios and heard those famous words: "The *Eagle* has landed." Of course, it wasn't an eagle that landed on the moon—it was humans.

The astronauts then made a lot of very careful preparations, put on their space suits, and at 39 minutes

and 35 seconds past 2 a.m. on July 21, they opened the spacecraft door. After some more preparations, Armstrong started climbing down the ladder, which had exactly nine rungs.

At 56 minutes and 15 seconds past 2 a.m., Armstrong stepped off the last rung of the ladder, placed his boots on the surface of the moon, and declared, **"That's one small step for man, one giant leap for mankind."**

We know every tiny detail of this event.

The Stone Age must have been full of great historical events too. For example, what happened when a Sapiens tribe first entered a valley inhabited by Neanderthals? The next few years probably saw many dramatic scenes—just as important as the moon landing. But no one wrote down the stories of these events because Stone Age people couldn't write. Over time, all the stories were forgotten. That's why we've never heard about these events, even though they must have happened.

We can try to imagine what happened: maybe it all started with a woman who climbed a hill to pick strawberries and saw some strange humans in the valley below. She came running back, screaming, "Monsters! Monsters!"

Her band told people from other bands about the monsters, and they all agreed to meet on the night of the next full moon to decide what to do. On that night, people from all the different bands gathered around the campfire and talked one by one, their faces lit by the flames. Some people thought the Neanderthals weren't

monsters at all and suggested that they could be friends. Some said it was best just to stay away from them and not enter their valley. Others insisted that they were dangerous monsters and everyone should come together to fight them and conquer their valley. And no one could decide who was right.

So everybody agreed to ask the tribe's guardian spirits because they might know what to do. The tribe's spirit doctor—who knew all about the tribe's guardian spirits—organized a sacred dance, with beating drums and stomping feet. The tribe danced and danced, calling on the guardian spirits for help, until finally the spirit doctor heard the spirits' voices clearly whispering, "War." (But you never know—maybe the spirit doctor didn't really hear anything. It was just that the people who wanted war had promised him 100 ivory beads and three fox-tooth hats if he said he heard "war." So he lied.)

Then came the battle, with wooden clubs and stone-tipped spears. And it was a massacre. There were no Neanderthals left. Except for one frightened three-year-old boy, found hiding under a thorny bush. One kind Sapiens offered to adopt the boy, but other people objected furiously, shouting that the boy was a monster and should be killed. There was another tense discussion around the campfire, with flashing eyes and raised voices. Soon people were drawing their clubs and spears and waving them around. Just as they were about to start fighting, the oldest member of the tribe, who rarely said a word, got up, took off her deerskin cloak, and put it around the boy's shoulders. And so the boy stayed. He grew up to be a member of the Sapiens tribe, and his blood still runs in our veins today. Perhaps he's your ancestor!

But all this is just imagination, not facts. Maybe it really happened like that, and maybe it was completely different. Maybe there was no war, no battle, no massacre at all. Maybe when Sapiens first met Neanderthals, they

had a big party together, with everybody dancing, singing, exchanging fox-teeth hats, and even kissing. People were still telling stories about that wonderful party many years later. But eventually it was forgotten, like everything else that happened in the Stone Age.

We don't know what really happened because **we just don't have enough evidence.** At most, archaeologists might find a fox tooth from somebody's hat, and scientists might find a Neanderthal gene in your DNA. The tooth and the gene can tell us a few things about our Stone Age ancestors. But they mostly remain silent when it comes to details of particular events. The fox tooth can't tell us whether it belonged to a hat worn in war or a hat for a party.

Like that first encounter between Sapiens and Neanderthals, there are countless other Stone Age dramas hidden from us behind a thick curtain of silence. **This curtain veils tens of thousands of years of history.** And in that time, there might have been many wars and parties, people may have followed all kinds of religions and philosophies, and artists could have composed the best songs ever. But we don't know anything about any of them.

There is one thing, though, we are certain our ancestors did, and it's something we know a lot about: they caused most of the world's big animals to disappear.

4

WHERE DID ALL THE
ANIMALS GO?

50 million years ago (*Pakicetus*)

48 million years ago (*Ambulocetus*)

33 million years ago (*Dorudon*)

27 million years ago (*Toipahautea waitaki*)

WHALE
GRANDPA

IN THE BEGINNING, HUMANS DIDN'T LIVE ALL OVER THE world—only in some parts. Our Sapiens ancestors lived in Africa, Neanderthals lived in Europe and the Middle East, Denisovans lived in Asia, and the small humans of Flores Island lived on Flores Island.

In many other parts of the world, there were no humans at all. There were no humans in America or in Australia or on many islands like Japan, New Zealand, Madagascar, and Hawaii.

This is because humans were not very good swimmers. They could sometimes reach islands, like Flores, that were really close to the mainland, but they couldn't cross the open sea to reach places like Australia or Hawaii.

When our Sapiens ancestors left Africa some 70,000 years ago, they started out by walking everywhere. They walked to Europe, where they met the Neanderthals;

they walked to Asia, where they met the Denisovans; and they walked on and on until they reached the farthest end of Asia . . . and couldn't walk any farther. But that didn't stop them because they now had a great idea. They knew that wood floats on water, so they tied logs together to make rafts, or they hollowed out tree trunks to make canoes—and they went to sea.

This was an amazing achievement. There are other animals that started out living on land and then evolved to live in the sea. For example, the ancient ancestors of whales were land animals that were no bigger than a large dog. Around 50 million years ago, some of these doglike animals started spending part of their time in rivers and lakes, hunting fish and other small creatures. Scientists discovered the skeleton of one of these animals in Pakistan, and they called it *Pakicetus*. The descendants of *Pakicetus* adapted to living in water; they spent more and more of their time in rivers, rarely venturing onto land. Their feet, which they no longer needed for walking, evolved into flippers. Their tails also changed to better help with swimming. Eventually, these animals swam out to sea: completely abandoning land, they spent their whole lives deep in the ocean. And their bodies adapted, growing enormous, until they became whales.

But this process took millions and millions of years. Not one of the animals felt the change during its own lifetime. Not one of them started life as a small land animal and grew up to become a giant whale in the ocean. And none of them felt that they were a quarter-whale or a half-whale. At every step along the way, they were what they were, and that was good enough for them. If one of those doglike whale ancestors met a present-day whale, it would never guess that this giant sea monster was its relative.

And whales are probably not the last step either. They might continue to evolve, and who knows what they'll look like in 50 million years!

Unlike whales, Sapiens didn't have to wait for their bodies to evolve when they wanted to cross the sea; they just invented new tools. They didn't start growing flippers; they started building boats. And it didn't take them millions of years; it took just a few generations.

When Sapiens first learned to build boats, they rowed to islands they could see from the shore. Then they rowed on, from one island to another, until they reached the farthest island. They couldn't see any more islands in the distance. Maybe this was the end of the world?

But they didn't stop there. Perhaps some adventurous people said that there might be more islands hiding beyond the horizon. "How do you know there are more islands?" their cautious friends asked. "You haven't seen them."

"How do you know there *aren't* more islands?" they replied. "You haven't been there."

Anyway, a group of people must have decided to take the risk and sail into the unknown to see for themselves. They loaded as much food and water as they could onto their rafts and into their canoes and started rowing. And they rowed and rowed, until they could no longer see the island where their brave journey started . . . but they still couldn't see any new islands in the distance. And now their food and water were running low. If they went any farther, they might not have enough provisions to make the journey back. What would you do if you were in one of those boats?

Some of the adventurers probably thought it was too dangerous and turned back. But others decided to go on. Maybe one of them saw a bird flying up ahead and thought, "That bird must be going somewhere, so there must be land ahead!" And on they rowed. And on. And on.

Until they finally reached Australia.

That was about 50,000 years ago. The journey made by the first people to reach Australia is one of the most important events in history. It's even more important than Columbus's journey to America, or the journey Neil Armstrong and his friends made to the moon. The moment when the first humans set foot on an Australian beach was the moment when we humans became the most dangerous animal in the world—the rulers of planet Earth. Until then, humans had had a relatively small influence on their environment, but from that moment onward, they started completely changing the world.

AUSTRALIA'S
GIANTS

When those first humans landed on that beach, they didn't know anything about Australia. Have you ever moved to a new town or a new school? It can be difficult, right? You don't know who the nice kids are and who the bullies are. If you see a teacher coming toward you in the corridor, you don't know if you should say good morning or just get out of the way. You don't know where the best drinking fountain is or where the coolest kids hang out.

It felt a bit like that for the first humans who reached Australia. No human had ever been there before, so they knew nothing about the place. They didn't know which mushrooms and berries were good to eat and which were poisonous. If a kangaroo came toward them, they couldn't be sure if it was dangerous or harmless. They didn't know where to find water holes and flint stones. Everything was new.

As they started exploring their new home, they discovered all sorts of huge, strange animals. At the time, Australia didn't have just the kangaroos that we know today. There were also kangaroos that reached a height of over six feet and weighed 400 pounds. These giant kangaroos were hunted by a kind of kangaroo-lion hybrid called a *thylacoleo*, or pouch lion. Pouch lions were big and fierce like lions and had a pouch like a kangaroo's to carry their offspring. Huge flightless birds called *genyornis* ran across the plains of Australia. They were bigger than humans and laid huge eggs—you could make a giant omelet from just one egg!

Giant koalas lived in the forests, dragon-like

Giant moa

Wonambi

Procoptodon

Megalania

Extinct giants from around the world

lizards warmed themselves in the sun, and sixteen-foot-long snakes slithered through the grass. These snakes could probably eat three kids at once and still have room in their stomachs for more! The biggest animal of all was called a *diprotodon*. These enormous wombat-like creatures weighed almost three tons and were the size of an SUV.

Soon after Sapiens reached Australia, all these huge animals became extinct—and many small animals did too. To become extinct means to disappear . . . totally, utterly, completely. When an animal becomes extinct, every animal of that particular kind dies. Once they're all dead, there can't be any new ones, so that animal is gone forever. This is what happened to the giant kangaroos, the pouch lions, the sixteen-foot snakes, the *diprotodons*, and many other animals. But why?

When something bad happens and you know that it's your fault, it's very tempting to blame somebody else. You played ball in the living room and your mother's

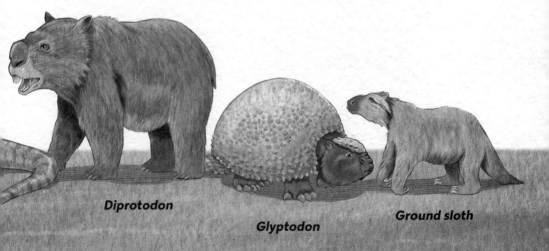

Diprotodon

Glyptodon

Ground sloth

favorite vase broke? Of course the cat did it! Well, in the same way, some people claim that Australia's giant animals became extinct because the climate in Australia changed. It grew colder and there was less rain, so there wasn't enough food for the animals, and they died.

Now, that's really hard to believe. It's true that the Australian climate changed about 50,000 years ago, but it wasn't a major change. In any case, these big animals had been living in Australia for millions of years and managed to survive many previous changes in the climate. Why did they suddenly disappear exactly when the first humans arrived? Let's be honest and accept the truth: the most plausible explanation is that the **Sapiens caused the extinction** of all these animals.

But how could ancient Sapiens cause such a disaster? They didn't have guns and bombs. They didn't drive cars and trucks. They didn't build cities and factories. They only had Stone Age tools. But they did have three big advantages: cooperation, the element of surprise, and the ability to control fire.

Their first advantage was that they could tell stories that brought many people together. Before Sapiens came to Australia, the big local predators, such as the pouch lions, usually hunted alone or in very small groups. But when Sapiens went hunting, they could get many people to cooperate. A huge *diprotodon* could defend herself from a single pouch lion, but not from twenty cunning Sapiens. Even more importantly, Sapiens could share information in ways that pouch lions couldn't. If people in one band developed a new trick to hunt *diprotodons*, they could quickly teach their trick to all the other bands. And if one person discovered where the *genyornis* birds usually laid their huge eggs, soon everybody in the neighborhood knew about it too.

Sapiens had already learned to hunt in groups and to share information when they lived in Africa and Asia. When they came to Australia, they gained another important advantage: the element of surprise. Humans had lived in Africa and Asia for 2 million years, gradually improving their hunting methods. At first, the animals of Africa and Asia didn't worry about humans much, but over time they learned to be afraid of them. By the time Sapiens developed their unique ability to cooperate in large numbers, animals in Africa and Asia already knew to keep well away from humans. They knew that two-legged apes with sticks in their hands meant trouble: they'd better run, and fast! But the animals in Australia had no time to adjust to humans.

The thing about humans is that we don't look particularly dangerous. We don't have big muscular bodies like tigers, long sharp teeth like alligators, or huge horns like rhinoceroses, and we can't run fast like cheetahs. So when a giant Australian *diprotodon* saw these two-legged apes from Africa for the first time, the *diprotodon* gave them one glance, shrugged, and went back to chewing leaves. These strange new creatures didn't seem like a threat. How could they possibly hurt a *diprotodon*?

The truth is that humans were already the deadliest animals on earth. Far, far more dangerous than any lion or any sixteen-foot snake. Of course, a single human is much less dangerous than a single lion or snake. But 100 Sapiens working together can do things that lions and snakes can't. Hunting *diprotodons* and Australia's other large animals was even easier than hunting African and Asian elephants and rhinos because the Australian animals didn't bother trying to escape when they saw humans coming. That's why all of Australia's *diprotodons* disappeared, while some of the elephants and rhinos managed to survive in Africa. The poor *diprotodons* became extinct before they learned to be afraid of humans.

This may sound strange, but it takes time to learn fear. We usually think of fear as something that we feel automatically, right? But think about the things you find scary. What do you find scarier: a big hairy spider or a car? If you're like most people, when you see a big hairy spider creeping toward you, you turn around and run

away. Maybe you even scream, "Ahhh! Spider!" But you don't run away every time you see a car. Why not? Every year, cars kill more than a million people . . . while spiders hardly kill anyone.

But spiders were already around in the Stone Age, whereas cars were invented just a century ago. So humans had time to learn to be afraid of spiders, but they haven't had time to become afraid of cars. It was exactly like that with the poor *diprotodons*. Maybe they were afraid of big hairy spiders too, but they weren't afraid of the most dangerous thing around—humans.

So, humans could cooperate, they had the element of surprise, and they had a third big advantage: **they controlled fire.** When Sapiens reached Australia, they already knew how to start a fire anywhere and anytime they wanted. When they came to a dense forest full of strange animals, they didn't have to hunt them one by one and risk being trampled by an angry *diprotodon*. Instead, they could start a fire and burn down the entire forest.

The humans could wait outside the forest for the frightened animals to run straight into a trap. Or they could just wait for the forest to burn with the animals inside it, and when the flames died down, they could help themselves to a lot of roasted *diprotodon* and kangaroo.

That's how the Sapiens killed all of Australia's giant animals. **Not even one survived.** Humans completely changed Australia, and it was the first time they did that— the first time that they totally changed a part of the world.

THE DISCOVERY OF
AMERICA

The thing about bad habits is that it's so hard to get rid of them. They tend to stay with you wherever you go. Unfortunately, **our ancestors were no exception to this rule.** Wiping out so many of Australia's animals was the first big thing they did. The second big thing was to wipe out animals in America.

Reaching America was more difficult than reaching Australia. America is separated from Africa and Europe by the Atlantic Ocean, which is huge; it's separated from Asia by the Pacific Ocean, which is even bigger. Only the northern tip of America, called Alaska, comes close to the northern tip of Asia, called Siberia. In fact, until about 10,000 years ago, the sea level was so low that you could actually walk from Siberia to Alaska, so you didn't need to cross any water.

But the climate in this Arctic region was extremely cold. In northern Siberia, temperatures could reach -58 degrees Fahrenheit in winter, and there were many days when the sun never came up. Even

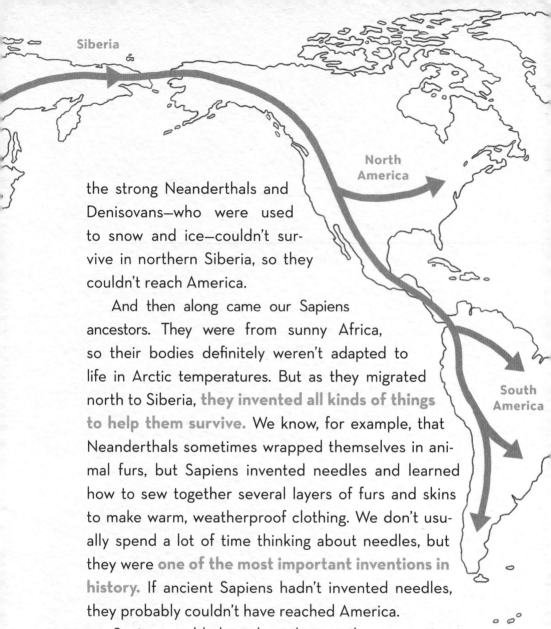

Siberia

North America

South America

the strong Neanderthals and Denisovans—who were used to snow and ice—couldn't survive in northern Siberia, so they couldn't reach America.

And then along came our Sapiens ancestors. They were from sunny Africa, so their bodies definitely weren't adapted to life in Arctic temperatures. But as they migrated north to Siberia, **they invented all kinds of things to help them survive.** We know, for example, that Neanderthals sometimes wrapped themselves in animal furs, but Sapiens invented needles and learned how to sew together several layers of furs and skins to make warm, weatherproof clothing. We don't usually spend a lot of time thinking about needles, but they were **one of the most important inventions in history.** If ancient Sapiens hadn't invented needles, they probably couldn't have reached America.

Sapiens could also rely on large-scale cooperation to hunt the big animals, such as mammoths, that lived in the Far North. Every mammoth they hunted was like an entire supermarket for them. It had tons of meat and fat—some mammoths weighed twelve tons! People couldn't eat this much meat at once, but they learned to preserve the meat by smoking it or by freezing it in the ice. They could use the mammoth's fur and skin to make thermal coats and shoes. They could use its larger bones to prop up their tents, and the smaller ones as tools. And they could use its ivory to make jewelry and art—like the lion-man statue or all the bracelets and beads found in Sunghir.

So, as winter drew near, perhaps an entire Sapiens tribe came together to hunt mammoths. They would then divide the meat, skin, and ivory among many small bands. Each group would also gather other kinds of food and collect as much wood as possible. When winter came, each group would retreat to a cave for shelter. As the sun disappeared and snowstorms swept the land, the band would stay in their cave, warming themselves around a blazing fire. To pass the time, they may have told stories about mammoths and ghosts and strange creatures that were half human and half lion. Perhaps they also told jokes and sang songs. They sewed coats from mammoth fur, made shoes from mammoth skin, and carved beads and jewelry from mammoth ivory. When they were hungry, they went to the coldest part of the cave—which served as their refrigerator—took a slice of mammoth steak, and cooked it over the fire. Obviously, they didn't have a real refrigerator running on electricity, but when temperatures dropped to –58 degrees Fahrenheit, every cave could become a natural refrigerator!

The ornate hats and belts found in Sunghir prove that mammoth hunters did more than just survive—they prospered. They multiplied and spread across the Far North, hunting mammoths, woolly rhinoceroses, and reindeer, and also fishing along the coast. When there were no mammoths or fish left in one place, they simply moved on, looking for more. Until one day, they crossed from Siberia to Alaska—and discovered America. Of course, they didn't know they were discovering America. The mammoths and people thought that Alaska was just a continuation of Siberia. From Alaska they kept going, moving south across the whole of America. Originally, they lived by hunting the big animals in the Far North and fishing along the coast. But Sapiens can change their way of life very quickly, and that's what they did in America. Whenever they reached a new place, they immediately learned everything they could about the local plants and animals, and then they invented new tricks, developed new tools, and adapted to the new conditions.

The great-grandchildren of the mammoth hunters from Siberia could have ended up as fishing communities living in the swamps of the Mississippi delta. They no longer wore heavy coats made of mammoth fur but walked about almost naked. They no longer tracked mammoth herds over the frozen tundra, instead making nets to catch fish in the river. They forgot the taste of mammoth steak and started to like crabmeat. Maybe they also stopped believing in the lion-man, and started telling stories about the Great Alligator Spirit that lived deep in the swamp.

Meanwhile, their cousins learned how to live in the Sonoran Desert in Mexico, where there were many coyotes but no alligators. Other relatives adapted to living in the jungles of Central America. Others made their home along the banks of the Amazon River, or high in the Andes Mountains, or on the open Pampas of Argentina. A few even reached the island of Tierra del Fuego, at the southern tip of South America. And it took them no more than a few thousand years to settle all these different places. This journey across America is proof that our ancestors had amazing abilities. No other animal ever managed to adapt to so many different places so quickly.

And almost everywhere they went in America, humans hunted the big animals. By this time, humans were even better at hunting than when they had landed in Australia. One method humans developed was to have several groups approaching the animals from different directions and coordinating their moves so that the animals were completely surrounded. This meant that even if the animals were faster than Sapiens, they couldn't escape. Another method was to approach the animals from only one side, but drive them toward a cliff or a deep river that they couldn't cross. A third method was to drive the animals toward a narrow gorge or a river crossing. The animals would think that they had an escape route and crowd into this narrow passage. But another group of Sapiens would be waiting to ambush them. When the animals were tightly packed together, the hunters would start shooting them with arrows, throwing spears at them, or rolling rocks onto them.

If the animals lived on an open plain without any cliffs, rivers, or gorges, Sapiens could work together to build an artificial trap. They erected barriers made of wood or stone and dug deep pits that they covered with branches and leaves. They would then come up behind the animals, making a lot of noise and waving their arms to drive them toward the barriers and pits. Sometimes it could take several bands of people many weeks to make the barriers and dig the pits, but if it worked, they could hunt an entire herd of animals in one morning. In a place called

Tultepec in Mexico, archaeologists found two large pits containing the bones of fourteen mammoths. Humans may have dug these pits and then chased the mammoths into them.

When humans first came to America, it was full of not only mammoths but other large elephant-like animals called mastodons. America also had beavers as big as basketball players, herds of horses and camels, saber-toothed tigers, and lions bigger than today's African lion. Other ancient American animals didn't look like any animal today, such as the *megatherium*, which weighed up to four tons and reached a height of nineteen feet. That's almost twice the height of an elephant!

Soon after the humans arrived, most of these big animals became extinct.

BIG TROUBLE

Are you wondering why the big animals were the ones to die out? Why did mammoths, *megatheriums*, and giant beavers disappear, while small beavers and rabbits are still here? Well, there are several reasons.

First, when Sapiens organized collective hunts, they focused on larger animals rather than small ones—you don't call together dozens of hunters to chase around after a few rabbits! If you divide ten rabbits among fifty

people, nobody gets very much to eat . . . but if you manage to hunt even a single mammoth, everybody gets to eat well. So it's worth the effort.

Second, a rabbit's best defense is to hide: it can hop into a burrow, or just sit quietly under a bush, and you can't see where it's gone. **It's much harder for mammoths to hide.** Of course, big animals don't usually rely on hiding to avoid predators; they rely on their size. A mammoth doesn't need to hide from a wolf or an eagle because it's too big to be attacked by them. But size didn't provide any protection from groups of Sapiens. Just the opposite—the biggest animals were the most attractive prey to human hunters. **That's why the big animals were in big trouble.**

Third, large animals disappeared because there were relatively few of them, and they bred slowly. Suppose an area of land had a population of a thousand mammoths. Every year twelve baby mammoths were born and ten mammoths died of old age or because of injuries or illness. So this mammoth population would grow by two every year. Then Sapiens arrived and started hunting the mammoths. Even if they managed to kill just three mammoths a year, that was enough to change the balance. Now the mammoth population would drop by one every year. You do the math: there were a thousand mammoths to start with, and every year there was one less, so how long would it take for those mammoths to become extinct? And just think how sad the last mammoth must have been all on her own.

With rabbits it was a very different story. A similar area of land might have had a population of 100,000 rabbits. And rabbits breed extremely quickly. Every year thousands of baby rabbits were born. So even if humans managed to catch a lot of rabbits, the rabbit population hardly declined. In the end there were a lot of humans and a lot of rabbits but no mammoths.

Why were our ancestors so cruel? Why did they completely wipe out the mammoths?

The thing is, they probably didn't mean to do it. They were just hungry, and their children were hungry, and they hunted a few mammoths every year because they needed something to eat. They didn't know the effect this would have over many, many years. We often do very impactful things without realizing what we're doing.

The mammoth hunters didn't think that by hunting three mammoths every year, they would eventually cause the complete extinction of mammoths. People lived no more than twenty or thirty years, and it was many centuries before the mammoths were extinct, so **nobody noticed what was happening.** At most, a nostalgic grandfather might have grumbled: "Pfft . . . the young these days, they don't know what it was like in the old days. When I was a kid, there were so many mammoths around! Hardly any left now." And even if he did say this, maybe nobody believed him. Do you always believe what your parents and grandparents say about their childhood, when there were no smartphones and no internet?

This is another example of that important law of life: small changes nobody notices accumulate over time and become big changes. At any particular time, there's only a tiny change that we can't see, so we think that everything's still the same. Even if we watch carefully for a whole day or a whole week, we don't see a change. But over time, the **tiny changes accumulate and become very big changes.** That's how you grow up, that's how a small land animal became a huge whale, and that's how hunting a few mammoths every year caused the mammoths to die out.

Actually, even the mammoths themselves probably didn't notice that they were disappearing. After all, just like humans, mammoths lived only for a few decades. No mammoth lived for 1,000 years. Obviously, a mammoth knew if her best friend died, but she couldn't know that soon all the mammoths in the world would disappear.

THE EXTINCTION
EXPRESS

Our ancestors caused the extinction of many kinds of animals, not only in Australia and America but all over the world. We've just seen that mammoths disappeared in America, but they were also wiped out in Europe and Asia, where they'd lived for millions of years. By 10,000 years ago, the only mammoths left anywhere were on a few small islands in the very cold Far North.

One of these islands, Wrangel Island, is in the Arctic Ocean about ninety-three miles north of the

Siberian coast. It's an extremely cold place. Even after Sapiens reached Siberia, they couldn't get to Wrangel, so mammoths continued to live peacefully on the island for thousands of years after they disappeared from America, Europe, and Asia.

But about 4,000 years ago, some Sapiens finally managed to get to Wrangel Island . . . and soon there were no more mammoths at all.

The extinction of the mammoths affected many other animals and plants. That's another important law of life: animals and plants depend on one another, so if something happens to one kind of creature, it usually influences many others. And this law even applies to you. You influence many animals and plants in your neighborhood. Maybe you trample weeds on the way to the bus station. Maybe you also eat cookies on the way to the bus station, leaving behind a trail of crumbs that ants and sparrows find and eat. Maybe you clean cobwebs from the ceiling of your room. So if you move to another town, the spiders will probably be happy, but the ants and sparrows won't like it at all.

The same thing happens on a much larger scale with all animals. Think of bees, for example. Bees fly from flower to flower, and that's how flowers get their pollen to one another to make seeds. If some disaster kills all the bees, the flowers won't be able to spread their pollen and produce seeds. If there are no seeds, there can't be any new plants. If there are no plants, all the animals that eat plants—like rabbits—will die. If there are no rabbits, all the animals that eat rabbits—like foxes—will also die. That's how the extinction of one animal can affect many others. If you kill all the bees, the foxes will die too.

Mammoths were very important for lots of other plants and animals. When the mammoths were around, the weather was colder in the Arctic regions of the Far North, but these places still had many more plants and animals than they do today. Why was that? Well, it was thanks to the mammoths. In winter, when everything was covered with snow and ice, mammoths acted like snow-plows. They used their enormous strength and huge tusks to plow through the snow and uncover grass trapped underneath. They ate some of that grass, but there was enough left to feed smaller animals like arctic hares. And the arctic hares were eaten by arctic foxes.

By springtime, most of the frozen grass was eaten, leaving bare earth. This was a very good thing, because when the sun started warming the earth again, new plants could immediately grow, and these new plants provided food for the animals.

When mammoths became extinct, no animal was strong enough to plow the snow in winter and uncover the grass. So the other animals had nothing to eat. And because nobody was eating the frozen grass, it was difficult for new plants to grow when spring came. They were trapped under last year's dead grass. So now there was even less food for the animals. That's why when the mammoths were gone, the arctic hares and arctic foxes suffered too.

Sapiens didn't know any of this. The problem with Sapiens wasn't that they were evil; the problem was that they were too good at what they did. When they started hunting mammoths, they became so good at it that no mammoths survived. So they went on to hunt elk. But they were very good at that too, and very soon the elk also started to disappear.

When archaeologists dig down into the ground, they find the same story all over the world. Deep, deep down, they find evidence of many different kinds of animals, but no evidence of Sapiens. A little higher up, they find the first traces of Sapiens: perhaps a human bone, a tooth, or a spearpoint. And higher still is a layer with a lot of human remains, but no trace of the animals that were once there.

So step 1: lots of animals, no Sapiens. Step 2: Sapiens appear. Step 3: lots of Sapiens, no animals.

This happened in Australia. It happened in America, Asia, and Europe. And it happened on almost every island that humans discovered, like the island of Madagascar. For millions of years, this island was isolated from the rest of the world, so a lot of unique animals evolved there. These included giant lemurs, which could be bigger than gorillas. There were also elephant birds, which looked a little like ostriches and likewise couldn't fly. Standing ten feet tall and weighing almost half a ton, they were the largest birds in the world—not the kind of bird you'd like to meet in your backyard. These elephant birds and giant lemurs, along with most of the other large animals of Madagascar, suddenly vanished about 1,500 years ago—precisely when the first human farmers set foot on the island.

Similar disasters occurred on almost every one of the thousands of islands from the Pacific Ocean to the Mediterranean Sea. Even on the smallest islands, archaeologists found evidence of birds, insects, and snails that had lived there for thousands of years but suddenly vanished when the first humans arrived.

Only a few extremely remote islands have remained free from humans, and these islands still have some very interesting animals living on them today. The most famous example is the Galápagos Islands, which are home to giant tortoises. Just like Australia's *diprotodons*, these giants show no fear of humans.

Perhaps if we all understood just how many animals we've already driven to extinction, we'd do more to protect those that still survive. If we're not careful, we'll wipe out lions, elephants, dolphins,

and whales, the way our ancestors wiped out mammoths and *diprotodons*. The only big creatures left in the world will be humans—plus our pets and farm animals. There won't be any wild animals at all.

USE YOUR
SUPERPOWER!

When our ancestors caused the extinction of the mammoths and *diprotodons*, they didn't know what they were doing. **But we can't use that excuse today.** We know what we're doing to lions, elephants, whales, and dolphins. We're responsible for their future. And no matter how young you are, you can do something about it. Remember, even as a kid, **you're already more powerful than any lion or whale!** Sure, whales are much bigger

than you are, but you have the superpower of telling stories and cooperating.

The blue whale is the largest animal that ever existed. It's even longer and heavier than the biggest dinosaurs! It can reach a length of up to 100 feet and a weight of more than 150 tons. One whale weighs as much as 5,000 kids. And yet whales can't protect themselves against humans because **humans have learned to tell stories and cooperate in very sophisticated ways,** which whales can't understand.

A thousand years ago, whales were hunted by small groups of fishermen who sailed in flimsy wooden boats and used wooden spears. Whales could sometimes escape these boats, or even break them and sink them. But in the modern age, humans learned to cooperate in a new way: they started creating corporations.

Do you remember the corporations we talked about, like McDonald's? Well, McDonald's specializes in burgers

and fries, but some corporations specialized in whaling. These corporations bought large iron ships, and they equipped them with sonar to scan the ocean and with powerful cannons that could fire long distances. Now the whales couldn't hide, escape, or sink the ships. And even if one ship sank and the men on it drowned, the corporations just bought new ships and hired new sailors. **The whales couldn't sink the corporations, because they didn't even know corporations existed.** How can you protect yourself from something you can't see, hear, or smell—something that exists only in another animal's imagination?

So the corporations hunted more and more whales, and made more and more money. Fifty years ago, blue whales almost disappeared—just like the mammoths. Luckily, some humans noticed what was happening and

decided to save the whales. Being humans themselves, they understood what money is and how corporations work, so they knew what to do. They wrote letters to newspapers, they signed petitions to politicians, and they organized demonstrations. They told people not to buy products from corporations that hunted whales, and they asked governments to forbid whaling. **Many of the people who did all this were kids.**

One of those kids was an eleven-year-old American boy called Kenneth Gormly. One day in 1968, he saw several fishing boats surrounding a group of whales. The fishermen were using steel nets, divers, and even a sea-plane to spot and trap the whales. This group of whales included a mother and her baby. The mother managed to make a hole in the net and escape, but the steel

mesh cut her and she started bleeding. The baby whale couldn't follow her out and stayed trapped in the net. **Kenneth heard the mother and baby calling to each other,** and he watched as the fishermen caught the baby in the net and hauled him up into the boat. The baby whale called and cried to his mother, and the mother followed the boat, but she couldn't rescue her baby.

Kenneth was very upset by what he saw and heard, so when he got home, **he wrote down the whole story** and sent it to his local newspaper. The newspaper published his story, and later it was even read at a public meeting. Many adults who heard what Kenneth wrote suddenly understood how terribly whales were suffering.

It took more time and a lot more articles, letters, and demonstrations, but in the end the pressure worked: governments around the world eventually passed laws

and signed agreements to stop whaling. **The blue whale was saved, at least for a while.** But the blue whale is still in danger today, and so are many other animals. Whales and other animals can't protect themselves. They can't write articles for newspapers, send letters, or put pressure on governments. But you can. If you understand how corporations work, and if you know how to post a story on Instagram or organize a demonstration, you can help save whales and other animals. From a whale's point of view, you can do so many amazing things that **you almost seem like a superhero.**

THE MOST DANGEROUS ANIMAL
IN THE WORLD

So that's how we humans became the rulers of planet Earth. And how we came to hold the fate of all other animals in our hands. Even before humans built the first city, invented the wheel, and learned how to write, we had already spread all over the world and killed about half of all large land animals. Humans were the first animals in the history of our planet to reach almost all the different continents and islands, and we managed to change the entire world all by ourselves.

Our ancestors did all this thanks to their unique

abilities: **inventing stories and cooperating in large numbers.** This meant that our kind of human was far more powerful than Neanderthals or lions and elephants. It made us the most dangerous animal in the world.

So now you know the story of our ancient ancestors. You know why you sometimes wake up in the middle of the night frightened that there's a monster under the bed, why it's so nice sitting around a campfire watching the flames flicker, and why you want to eat a whole chocolate cake even though it isn't really good for you.

You know how a single finger bone can help identify a whole different kind of human. You know that some islands were once inhabited only by small humans and animals. You know that in the Stone Age, most tools were not made of stone and most people didn't live in caves. You know that teenagers and little girls can sometimes make important scientific discoveries. And you know that if you invent a good story that enough people believe, **you can conquer the world.**

You also know that there's so much we still don't know. We don't know what Neanderthals did with their giant brains. We don't know whether Sapiens and Neanderthals sometimes fell in love or what families were like in the Stone Age. We don't know what kind of religions people practiced back then.

And there are other questions. This book explained how our ancestors became the most powerful animal in the world; how they spread all over the planet, causing the Neanderthals, the Denisovans, and several other kinds of humans to disappear; and how they drove many of the world's animals to extinction. But even after doing all that, our ancestors still couldn't build cars, airplanes, and spaceships. They still didn't know how to write. They still didn't have farms and cities. They couldn't even grow wheat and make bread. So how did they learn to do all these things? **That's a whole other story.**

ACKNOWLEDGMENTS

It takes a community to raise a child. It also takes a community to create a book.

When you look at a book's cover, you usually see only the author's name in big letters. So you might imagine that just one person wrote the book. Maybe the author sat in their room for a year, wrote everything down—and there you are! A new book is out!

In reality, it is very different. So many people in so many places have worked hard on the book, doing lots of things the author couldn't do, or doesn't even know how to do. Without their contributions, there would be no book.

To type a sentence usually takes just a few seconds. But it actually took many weeks to write some of the sentences in this book. People had to check that we got the facts right. One month they were busy reading scientific papers about Neanderthals, and the next month it was all about whales.

Other people thought hard about the exact message of the sentence: Is it really what we want readers to know about history? Could it be misinterpreted? Might it hurt somebody? And then more people worked on the style. Is the sentence clear? Could it be made clearer?

And it was the same with the illustrations. Some illustrations were done ten times, going back and forth, sketching something and throwing it in the bin, drawing something and then redrawing it again and again. It should be a boy. No, make it a girl. Perhaps a bit younger? No, that's too young....

So writing a single sentence or drawing a single illustration could involve lots of emails and phone calls and meetings. And somebody had to coordinate all those emails and phone calls and meetings. And then there were contracts to sign and salaries to pay, and don't forget the food—nobody can do anything unless they eat, right?

So I would like to thank all the people who helped create this book. I could never have done it without them.

Ricard Zaplana Ruiz drew the wonderful illustrations that bring human history to life.

Jonathan Beck enthusiastically supported the project and helped bring it to fruition.

Susanne Stark taught me how to see the world from the perspective of young people, and how to write more simply, more clearly, and more deeply than I thought I could.

Sebastian Ullrich meticulously read and reread every word and made sure that in our attempt to write an engaging and accessible story, we did not compromise on scientific accuracy.

Then there are the wonderful people of the Sapienship team: Naama Wartenburg, Jason Parry, Daniel Taylor, Michael Zur, Nina Zivy, Shay Abel, Guangyu Chen, Hannah Morgan, Galiete Gothelf, Nadav Neuman, Hannah Yahav, and Ettie Sabag, with the additional support from the very talented copy editor, Adriana Hunter; the layout designer, Hanna Shapiro; and the diversity consultant, Slava Greenberg. All led by our dedicated and brilliant CEO, Naama Avital. Each and every team member contributed to this project. Without their professionalism, diligence, and creativity, there would have been no book.

I would also like to thank my mother, Pnina; my sisters, Einat and Liat; and my nieces and nephews, Tomer, Noga, Matan, Romi, and Uri, for their love and support.

My grandmother Fanny passed away at the age of 100 just as we were finishing the book. I will always be grateful for her unlimited kindness and joy.

And I would finally like to thank my husband, Itzik, who has dreamt about creating this book for years. He founded Sapienship to make this and other projects come to life and has been my inspiration and my loving companion for over two decades.

—Yuval Noah Harari

Thanks to all the fellow Homo sapiens of my profession for sharing their knowledge and friendship.

To Ada Soler and Rosa Samper for the vote of confidence.

To the team of professionals that make up Sapienship for their help and guidance in all the steps of the creation process.

And of course to Yuval Noah Harari for trusting my illustrations to travel halfway around the world with his text.

—Ricard Zaplana Ruiz

ABOUT THIS BOOK

The great thing about science is that it keeps finding new things. Every year, scientists make new discoveries that change how we understand the world. In this book, we've tried to rely on the latest scientific knowledge, but even scientists disagree on some things. And there are parts of human history that might always remain a mystery. But wait! That doesn't mean everything's debatable. We can say for sure that there used to be many different kinds of humans on this planet. We know that the only remaining kind of human—our kind—learned how to control plants and animals, built cities and empires, and invented space-ships, atom bombs, and computers. These revolutions created the world you're living in right now. And maybe one day you'll discover something that will change how all humans understand the world. . . .

YUVAL NOAH HARARI is a historian, philosopher, and the bestselling author of *Sapiens: A Brief History of Humankind*, *Homo Deus: A Brief History of Tomorrow*, *21 Lessons for the 21st Century*, and *Sapiens: A Graphic History*. His books have sold 40 million copies in 65 languages, and he is considered one of the world's most influential public intellectuals today. Born in Israel in 1976, Harari received his PhD from the University of Oxford in 2002, and is currently a lecturer at the Department of History in the Hebrew University of Jerusalem. In 2019, Harari co-founded Sapienship with his husband, Itzik Yahav. Sapienship is a social impact company with projects in the fields of entertainment and education, whose main goal is to focus the public conversation on the most important global challenges facing the world today.

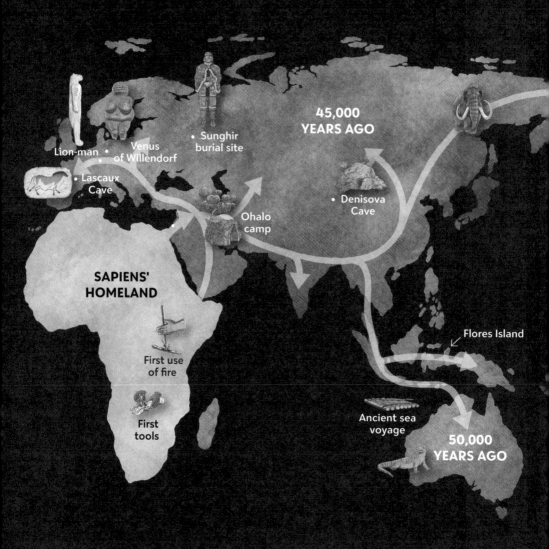

45,000 YEARS AGO

Lion-man

Venus of Willendorf

Sunghir burial site

Lascaux Cave

Ohalo camp

Denisova Cave

SAPIENS' HOMELAND

First use of fire

First tools

Flores Island

Ancient sea voyage

50,000 YEARS AGO

WORLD MAP OF
HISTORY

 Path of Sapiens' migration

15,000 YEARS AGO

Cave of the Hands